The Scarecrow Author Bibliographies

JOHN RUSKIN:
A Bibliography, 1900-1974

by

KIRK H. BEETZ

The Scarecrow Author Bibliographies, No. 28

The Scarecrow Press, Inc.
Metuchen, N.J.   1976

Library of Congress Cataloging in Publication Data

Beetz, Kirk H   1952-
    A bibliography of John Ruskin, 1900-1974.

    (The Scarecrow author bibliographies ; no. 28)
    Includes index.
    1.   Ruskin, John, 1819-1900--Bibliography.   I.
Title.
Z8765. B43   [PR5264]   016. 8288'09   76-13611
ISBN 0-8108-0938-9

LIBRARY
University of Texas
At San Antonio

CONTENTS

ACKNOWLEDGMENTS

Many thanks to Diane Johnson Murray, author, scholar, and professor, without whose inspirational teaching and willingness to help a student beyond the ordinary obligations of a teacher this bibliography would never have been begun and certainly never completed. Such generosity toward one who clearly can never repay it is a rare gift which I shall long remember. My thanks also to Theodore F. Gould, reference librarian at The University of California at Davis, who showed me the instruments a library can provide a bibliographer for his work. My thanks to Suzanne Munich for her proofreading of the Introduction and her advice about its content.

INTRODUCTION

     I have organized this compilation for ease of use. My intent has been to create a work which the beginning, as well as the advanced, John Ruskin scholar could utilize. Hence, the Table of Contents is organized in such a manner that one can easily find works in either a general area or a specific area. Criticism and scholarship published in periodicals, for instance, can be found in Part II, Periodicals, under the subdivision for Criticism and Scholarship (II. B). The latter section is divided into more specific areas for those who may have a more precise topic in mind.

     The beginning scholar should note that the standard reference collection of John Ruskin's works is The Works of John Ruskin (also known as The Library Edition of the Works of John Ruskin), edited by Edward Tyas Cook and Alexander Wedderburn; it is recommended for use in locating direct quotations from John Ruskin's works. One other work which is useful in this context is Praeterita, John Ruskin's autobiography, edited by Kenneth Clark. For John Ruskin's diaries, The Diaries of John Ruskin, edited by Joan Evans and John Howard Whitehouse, is the standard reference work. No one work can, at present, be regarded as the standard collection of John Ruskin's correspondence. The sections here, under Books and Periodicals, which deal with letters and correspondence, list works which can be used to supplement the letters collection in The Works of John Ruskin.

     If a specific scholar's works and opinions are desired, the reader should consult the Index at the back of this volume. Works which mention John Ruskin's name only fleetingly are not included in this volume.

With few exceptions, book reviews of secondary materials have also been omitted.

In the sections listing editions of Ruskin's works, each discrete edition is given a separate entry. In cases where the identical edition has been issued by two or more publishers, with no change except the imprint, these are combined within one entry. The arrangement of editions of the same work is chronological.

PART I

BOOKS

A. EDITIONS OF WORKS

1. Poetry, Essays, and Fiction

a. Editions devoted solely to Ruskin

1   The Art Criticism of John Ruskin. Ed. Robert L. Herbert. Gloucester, Mass.: Peter Smith, 1964. (paperback, New York: Doubleday, 1964.)

2   Best of Ruskin. Ed. A. E. Sims. New York: T. Y. Crowell, 1915.

3   The Cestus of Aglaia. Orpington: 1905. New York: E. P. Dutton, 1907. (Everyman's Library.)

4   Children's King of the Golden River. Ed. F. H. Lee. London: George G. Harrap, 1940.

5   Comments of John Ruskin on the Divina Commedia. Ed. George P. Huntington. Boston: Houghton Mifflin, 1903.

6   Complete Works. London: Eyre and Spottiswoode, 1930.

7   Crown of Wild Olive. New York: Peter Smith, 1935.

8   Crown of Wild Olive, and The Queen of the Air. Ed. Wightman F. Melton. New York: Macmillan, 1910.

9   Dame Wiggins of Lee and Her Seven Wonderful Cats.
    Ed. Francesca Marshall. Philadelphia: David Mc-
    Kay, 1929.
        John Ruskin is credited with editing and adding
        some verses to Dame Wiggins of Lee. Author-
        ship is generally credited to Richard Scrafton
        Sharpe and Mrs. Pearson.

10 _____. Akron, Ohio: Saalfield, 1929.

11 Dame Wiggins of Lee and Her Seven Wonderful
    Cats: A Humorous Tale Written Principally by a
    Lady of Ninety. New York: E. P. Dutton, 1928.

12 _____. New York: McGraw-Hill, 1963.

13 Dame Wiggins of Lee and Her Seven Wonderful
    Cats: A Humorous Tale Written Principally by a
    Lady of Ninety: Original Rhymes Made into a
    Primer for Children. Ed. Francesca Marshall.
    New York: Educational Publishing Company, 1908.
        See entry no. 9.

14 Dame Wiggins of Lee and Her Seven Wonderful
    Cats: A Humorous Tale Written Principally by a
    Lady of Ninety: A Famous Ballad, Told and Sung
    in England: in 1885 John Ruskin Wrote Some New
    Verses for It: in 1925 Roy Meldrum Made These
    New Pictures. New York: Macmillan, 1925.

15 Elements of Drawing. Saint Clair Shores, Mich.:
    Scholarly Press, 1970 (reprint of 1889 edition).

16 The Elements of Drawing. New York: Dover Pub-
    lications, 1971 (reprint from volume 15, 1904, of
    the Library Edition of The Works of John Ruskin).
        See Library Edition (entry no. 55).

17 The Elements of Drawing and The Elements of Per-
    spective. New York: E. P. Dutton, 1907. (Ev-
    eryman's Library.)

18 Ethics of the Dust. New York: E. P. Dutton,

1907. (Everyman's Library.)

19 Ethics of the Dust: Ten Lectures to Little House-
   wives on the Elements of Crystallization. Ed.
   R. O. Morris. London: Oxford University Press,
   1914.

20 Fors Clavigera: Letters to the Workmen and La-
   bourers of Great Britain. 4 vols. Westport,
   Conn.: Greenwood Press, 1968 (reprint of 8-vol-
   ume 1886 edition).

21 The Genius of John Ruskin: Selections from His
   Writings. New York: George Braziller, 1963.
   London: George Allen and Unwin, 1964. Boston:
   Houghton Mifflin, 1965.

22 Gothic Book-Plates: Being Certain Passages from
   "The Nature of Gothic," by John Ruskin, and Cer-
   tain Book-Plates by Bertha Gorst. Kansas City,
   Mo.: H. Alfred Fowler, 1912.

23 Iteriad or Three Weeks Among the Lakes. Ed.
   James S. Dearden. Newcastle upon Tyne: Frank
   Graham, 1969.

24 John Ruskin on Himself and Things in General.
   Folcroft, Pa.: Folcroft Library Editions, 1974
   (reprint of 1893 edition).

25 King of the Golden River. Philadelphia: John C.
   Winston, 1929.

26 _____. Boston: D. C. Heath, 1930.

27 _____. Philadelphia: J. B. Lippincott, 1932.
   (Limited edition published jointly by Harrap.)

28 _____. Ed. K. L. Bates. Chicago: Rand Mc-
   Nally, no date (circa 1932).

29 _____. London: Hutchinson, 1934.

30   _____ . Philadelphia: David McKay, 1935.

31   _____ . London: Blackie and Son, no date (circa 1937). (Blackie's Graded Story Readers, Grade 4.)

32   _____ . Chicago: Albert Whitman, no date (circa 1937).

33   _____ . London: George G. Harrap, 1939.

34   _____ . New York: Duell, Sloan and Pearce, 1945.

35   _____ . New York: The World Publishing Co., 1946.

36   _____ . Ann Arbor, Mich.: University Microfilms, 1966.

37 King of the Golden River: And Dame Wiggins of Lee and Her Seven Wonderful Cats. Philadelphia: J. B. Lippincott, 1921.

38   _____ . Philadelphia: John C. Winston, 1929.

39 King of the Golden River: or, The Black Brothers. Ed. M. V. O'Shea. Boston: D. C. Heath, 1900.

40   _____ . New York: Longmans, Green, 1914.

41   _____ . New York: T. Y. Crowell, no date (circa 1917).

42   _____ . Ed. Austin G. Schmidt. Chicago: Loyola University Press, 1918.

43   _____ . New York: Macmillan, 1926.

44   _____ . Chicago: Albert Whitman, 1927.

45   _____ . New York: W. E. Rudge, 1930.

46 _____ . New York: Macmillan, 1952.

47 _____ . London: Edmund Ward, 1958. Toronto: British Book Service, 1958. New York: Franklin Watts, 1959.

48 _____ . London: Hutchinson, 1961.

49 _____ . New York: Macmillan, 1963. Milan, Italy: Fratelli Fabbri, 1963.

50 _____ . New York: Franklin Watts, 1967.

51 The King of the Golden River: or, The Black Brothers: A Legend of Stiria. Boston: Ginn, 1916.

52 _____ . New York: Dover Publications, 1974.

53 King of the Golden River: or, The Black Brothers: with a Biographical Sketch, Notes and Portrait. Chicago: Beckley-Cardy, 1914.

54 The Lamp of Beauty: Writings on Art by John Ruskin. Ed. Joan Evans. London: Phaidon, 1959. New York: Doubleday, 1960.

55 The Library Edition of the Works of John Ruskin. 39 vols. Ed. Edward Tyas Cook and Alexander Wedderburn. London: George Allen, 1903-1912. See also The Works of John Ruskin (entry no. 142). Letters by John Ruskin are included.

56 The Literary Criticism of John Ruskin. Ed. Harold Bloom. Garden City, New York: Anchor Books (Doubleday), 1965. Gloucester, Mass.: Peter Smith, 1969. Abridged edition: New York: W. W. Norton, 1972.

57 Modern Painters. New York: E. P. Dutton, 1906. (Everyman's Library.)

58 _____ . 5 vols. Boston: Dana Estes, 1913.

59 _____. Boston: L. C. Page, no date (circa 1932).

60 Mornings in Florence. Boston: H. M. Caldwell, 1912.

61 Mornings in Florence: Being Simple Studies of Christian Art for English Travellers. Saint Clair Shores, Mich.: Scholarly Press, 1972 (reprint of 1907 edition).

62 Munera Pulveris: Six Essays on the Elements of Political Economy. Westport, Conn.: Greenwood Press, 1969 (reprint of 1891 edition).

63 Mystery of Life and Its Arts. New York: Oxford University Press, 1913.

64 Noble Thoughts of John Ruskin. Boston: L. C. Page, no date (circa 1937).

65 Of Queens' Gardens. New York: Hearst's International Library, 1915.

66 The Pheasant. Ed. James S. Dearden. Bembridge: The Yellowsands Press, 1965.

67 The Pigwiggian Chaunts of John Ruskin. Ed. James S. Dearden. Bembridge: The Yellowsands Press, 1960.

68 Poems. Ed. Gilbert Keith Chesterton. London: 1906.

69 The Poetry of Architecture: or, The Architecture of Nations of Europe Considered in Its Association with Natural Scenery and National Character. Saint Clair Shores, Mich.: Scholarly Press, 1972 (reprint of 1893 edition).

70 The Poetry of Architecture: or, The Architecture of the Nations of Europe. New York: Gordon Press, no date (circa 1974).

71 Political Economy of Art: Unto This Last: Sesame
    and Lilies: The Crown of Wild Olive. New York:
    Macmillan, 1912.

72 Praeterita: Outlines of Scenes and Thoughts Per-
    haps Worthy of Memory in My Past Life. Ed. Ken-
    neth Clark. London: Rupert Hart-Davis, 1949.
      This edition has been highly praised by Ruskin
      scholars.

73 Pre-Raphaelitism: Lectures on Architecture and
    Painting, Etc. London: J. M. Dent, 1906. New
    York: E. P. Dutton, 1906. (Everyman's Library.)

74 A Ride in Wales. Ed. James S. Dearden. Bem-
    bridge: The Yellowsands Press, 1964.

75 Ruskin: An Anthology. Ed. Kenneth Clark. New
    York: Roy, (1974).

76 Ruskin as Literary Critic. Ed. A. H. R. Ball.
    London: Cambridge University Press, 1928.

77 The Ruskin House Edition. 4 vols. London: E. P.
    Dutton, 1907. Everyman's Edition.

78 Ruskin on Pictures. Ed. Edward Tyas Cook. Lon-
    don: 1902.

79 Ruskin, the Painter, and His Works at Bembridge.
    Ed. John Howard Whitehouse. London: Oxford Uni-
    versity Press, 1938.

80 Ruskin Today. Ed. Kenneth Clark. London: J.
    Murray, 1964. New York: Holt, Rinehart and
    Winston, 1965.

81 Ruskin's Modern Painters. Ed. A. J. Finberg.
    London: G. Bell, 1927.

82 Saint Ursula. New York: Devin-Adair, 1912.

83 _____. New York: Paulist Press, 1926.

84 Selected Prose. Ed. Matthew Hodgart. New York:
    New American Library, 1972.

85 Selected Writings of John Ruskin. Ed. Peter Quen-
    nell. London: Falcon Press, 1952.

86 Selections and Essays. Ed. Frederick W. Roe.
    Philadelphia: Richard West, 1908. New York:
    Scribner's Sons, 1918. Saint Clair Shores, Mich.:
    Scholarly Press, 1971.

87 Selections from Ruskin. Ed. Arthur Christopher
    Benson. London: Macmillan, 1911. New York:
    Macmillan, 1923. London: Cambridge University
    Press, 1923.

88 Selections from "The Stones of Venice." Ed. E. A.
    Parlas. London: 1925.

89 Selections from the Works of John Ruskin. Ed.
    Chauncey Brewster Tinker. Boston: Houghton Mif-
    flin, 1912.

90 Selections Moral and Religious from the Works of
    John Ruskin. Ed. Frederick Webster Osborn. Bos-
    ton: Richard G. Badger (The Gorham Press), 1917.

91 Sesame and Lilies. Ed. Agnes Spofford Cook. New
    York: Silver, Burdett, 1900.

92 _____. Boston: Houghton Mifflin, 1900.

93 _____. Ed. Gertrude Buck. New York: Long-
    mans, Green, 1906.

94 _____. Ed. Charles Robert Gaston. Boston:
    D. C. Heath, 1909.

95 _____. Ed. G. G. Whiskard. New York: Ox-
    ford University Press, 1912.

96 _____. New York: T. Y. Crowell, 1912.

97 _____. New York: Barse and Hopkins, 1914.

98 _____. Ed. G. G. Whiskard. London: Oxford
University Press, 1914.

99 _____. Ed. Charles R. Rounds. New York:
American Book, 1916.

100 _____. Ed. Sybil Wragge. New York: E. P.
Dutton, 1920.

101 _____. Ed. J. W. Linn. Chicago: Scott,
Foresman, 1920.

102 _____. New York: Dodge, 1922.

103 _____. Ed. Lois G. Hufford. Boston: Ginn,
1927.

104 _____. Ed. Toong Zeubang. Shanghai: Com-
mercial Press, 1929.

105 _____. New York: Coward-McCann, (1932).

106 _____. Ed. G. E. Hollingworth. London: University Tutorial Press, 1932.

107 _____. New York: Thomas Nelson, 1933.

108 _____. New York: Peter Smith, 1935.

109 _____. Philadelphia: David McKay, 1941.

110 _____. New York: E. P. Dutton, (1974).

111 Sesame and Lilies and Ethics of the Dust. Ed.
G. G. Whiskard (Sesame and Lilies) and R. O.
Morris (Ethics of the Dust). London: Oxford Uni-
versity Press, 1914.

112 Sesame and Lilies, The Two Paths, and The King
of the Golden River. New York: E. P. Dutton,
1909.

113   Sesame and Lilies, The Two Paths, and The
      Oliver Lodge.   London: J. M. Dent and Sons,
      1953.

114   Seven Lamps of Architecture.   New York: E. P.
      Dutton, 1906.   (Everyman's Library, and non-
      series publication.)

115   _____.   New York: Longmans, Green, 1909.

116   _____.   London: J. M. Dent, 1913.

117   _____.   London: J. M. Dent, 1932.

118   _____.   London: J. M. Dent, 1956.   (Every-
      man's Library.)

119   _____.   New York: Farrar, Straus, and
      Giroux, (1974).

120   _____.   New York: E. P. Dutton, (1974).

121   The Seven Lamps of Architecture: Including Illus-
      trations Drawn and Etched by the Author.   New
      York: The Noonday Press, 1961.   Toronto: Am-
      bassador Books, 1961.

122   The Seven Lamps of Architecture: Lectures on
      Architecture and Painting: The Study of Architec-
      ture.   Boston: Estes, 190?.

123   Stones of Venice.   3 vols.   New York: E. P.
      Dutton, 1907.   (Everyman's Library.)

124   _____.   3 vols.   Boston: Dana Estes, 1913.

125   _____.   Ed. Joseph Gluckstein Links.   London:
      Collins, 1960.   New York: Hill and Wang, 1964
      (paperback, 1966).

126   The Stones of Venice: with Illustrations by John
      Ruskin.   New York: P. F. Collier, 1900.

127 Thoughts from Ruskin. Philadelphia: George W.
     Jacobs, 1912.

128 Time and Tide and Munera Pulveris. New York:
     Macmillan, 1928.

129 Time and Tide, Notes on the Construction of Sheep-
     folds, Lecture to the Cambridge School of Art.
     New York: E. P. Dutton, 1910. (Everyman's Li-
     brary.)

130 Turner. New York: George H. Doran, 1912.

131 Turner and Ruskin: An Exposition of the Work of
     Turner from the Writings of Ruskin. 2 vols. Ed.
     F. Wedmore. London: George Allen, 1900.

132 Two Boyhoods, and Other Select Passages. New
     York: E. P. Dutton, 1914. (Everyman's Library.)

133 Unto This Last. Ed. Susan Cunnington. New
     York: E. P. Dutton, 1921.

134 _____. New York: E. P. Dutton, (1974).
     Includes: "Political Economy of Art," and "Es-
     says of Political Economy."

135 Unto This Last, and Other Essays on Art and Po-
     litical Economy. New York: E. P. Dutton, 1907.
     (Everyman's Library.)

136 Unto This Last and Traffic. Ed. John L. Bradley.
     New York: Appleton-Century-Crofts, 1967.

137 Unto This Last: Four Essays on the First Prin-
     ciples of Political Economy. London: Allenson,
     (1937).

138 _____. Ed. Lloyd J. Hubenka. Lincoln, Neb.:
     University of Nebraska Press, 1967.

139 _____. Ed. P. M. Yarker. New York: Wil-
     liam Collins Sons, 1970.

140   Views of Social Justice. Ed. James Fuchs. New
       York: Vanguard Press, 1926.

141   A Walk in Chamouni and Other Poems. Ed. J. R.
       Tutin. London: Hull, 1908.

142   The Works of John Ruskin. 39 vols. Ed. Edward
       Tyas Cook and Alexander Wedderburn. New York:
       Longmans, Green, 1903-1912.
          See The Library Edition of the Works of John
          Ruskin, (entry no. 55). Letters by John Ruskin
          are included.

b.   Inclusions in works not devoted solely to Ruskin

143   "Art and History." Modern Reader: Essays on
       Present-Day Life and Culture. Ed. Walter Lipp-
       mann and Allan Nevins. Boston: Heath, 1936,
       pp. 595-600.

144   "At the Pantomime." Specimens of English Dra-
       matic Criticism, XVII - XX Centuries. Ed. Alfred
       Charles Ward. London: Oxford University Press,
       1945, pp. 130-131.

145   "Books." Essays Then and Now. Ed. Alice Celia
       Cooper and David Fallon. Boston: Ginn, 1937,
       pp. 264-269.

146   "Cambridge Inaugural Address." Essays Formal
       and Informal. Ed. Franklin William Scott and
       Jacob Zeitlin. New York: Ray Long and Richard
       R. Smith, 1930, pp. 125-149.

147   "Crown of Olives." Fifty Essays. Ed. Bergen
       Evans. Boston: Little, Brown, 1936, pp. 232-
       246.

148   "Crown of Wild Olive." A Selection from the Best

English Essays Illustrative of the History of English Prose Style. Ed. Sherwin Cody. Chicago: A. C. McClurg, 1903, pp. 360-375.

149 _____ . Essays of the Past and Present. Ed. Warner Taylor. New York: Harper, 1927, pp. 60-71.

150 _____ . Essays for Our Day: A Background of Models. Ed. Louis Byron Shackelford and Florien Preston Gass. New York: W. W. Norton, 1931, pp. 130-140.

151 "Early Education at Herne Hill." English Prose: A Series of Related Essays for the Discussion of the Art of Writing. Ed. Frederick William Roe and George Roy Elliott. New York: Longmans, Green, 1913, pp. 17-27.

152 "Entry Into Venice." Great English Essayists. Ed. William James Dawson and Coningsby William Dawson. New York: Harper, 1909, pp. 283-288. Reprinted: New York: H. W. Wilson, circa 1974.

153 "Extension of Railways in the Lake District." Book of English Essays (1600-1900). Ed. Stanley Victor Makower and Basil H. Blackwell. London: Oxford University Press, 1912, pp. 315-322.

154 "Extract from the 'Introduction' to 'A Crown of Wild Olive'." Types and Times in the Essay. Ed. Warner Taylor. New York: Harper, 1932, pp. 68-70.

155 "Extract from 'The Mystery of Life and Its Arts'." Types and Times in the Essay. Ed. Warner Taylor. New York: Harper, 1932, pp. 74-77.

156 "Extract from 'The Nature of Gothic,' Stones of Venice." Types and Times in the Essay. Ed. Warner Taylor. New York: Harper, 1932, pp. 71-73.

157   "Fors Clavigera, Letter V." Essays in Science
       and Engineering: Selected Readings for Students
       of Composition. Ed. Franz Montgomery. New
       York: Ray Long and Richard R. Smith, 1932, pp.
       49-63. Revised edition: Ed. Franz Montgomery
       and Luther N. Becklund. New York: Farrar and
       Rinehart, 1938, pp. 56-68.

158   "How Architecture Expresses a People's Soul."
       Points of View for College Students. Ed. Paul
       Kaufman. New York: Doubleday, Doran, 1926,
       pp. 193-221.
           The essay was originally entitled "Traffic."

159   "Idealist's Arraignment of the Age." English Es-
       says. Ed. Walter Cochrane Bronson. New York:
       Holt, Rinehart and Winston, 1905, pp. 259-272.

160   "John Ruskin." Prose of the Victorian Period.
       Ed. William E. Buckler. Boston: Houghton Mif-
       flin, 1958, pp. 345-405.
           Includes excerpts from Modern Painters (vol.
       III, part IV, chapter 3), The Stones of Venice
       (vol. II, chapter 6), Unto This Last (essay I).

161   "John Ruskin Bemoans the Degradation of Modern
       Life." Treasury of the World's Great Speeches.
       Ed. Houston Peterson. New York: Simon and
       Schuster, 1954, pp. 544-549.

162   King of the Golden River. London: Oxford Uni-
       versity Press, 1939. (With Magic Fishbone by
       Charles Dickens.)

163   _____. London: Golden Galley Press, 1946.
       (With Rip Van Winkle by Washington Irving.)

164   King of the Golden River, A Dog of Flanders, and
       Other Stories by Louise de la Ramée. New York:
       A. L. Burt, 1932.

165   King of the Golden River, A Dog of Flanders by
       Louise de la Ramée and Other Stories. New York:

Grosset and Dunlap, 1938.

166   The King of the Golden River and Cuore: Edited
      to Fit the Interests and Abilities of Young Readers.
      2 vols. Ed. Edward L. Thorndike. New York:
      Appleton-Century, 1936.
          Cuore was written by Edmondo de Amicis.

167   King of the Golden River, and Letting Off Steam:
      An Adaptation from Ruskin, and An Episode in the
      Life of James Watt. Ed. Norma T. Carrington.
      London: Herbert Russell, 1938.

168   King of the Golden River: or, The Black Brothers.
      Akron, Ohio: Saalfield, 1926. (With Pied Piper of
      Hamlin by Robert Browning.)

169   King of the Golden River: or, The Black Brothers
      and Other Wonder Stories, In the Amanuensis Style
      of Phonography by Jerome B. Howard. Cincinnati:
      Phonographic Institute, 1918.

170   "Lamp of Memory." Essays in Contemporary
      Civilization. Ed. Charles Wright Thomas. Lon-
      don: Macmillan, 1931, pp. 261-272.

171   _____ . Classic Essays in English. Ed. Jose-
      phine Miles. Boston: Little, Brown, 1961, pp.
      187-191.

172   "Lamp of Obedience." Essays and Studies: Prose
      Selections for College Reading. Ed. Frederick
      Miller Smith. Boston: Houghton Mifflin, 1922,
      pp. 145-156.

173   "Leafage of Trees." English Prose: A Series of
      Related Essays for the Discussion of the Art of
      Writing. Ed. Frederick William Roe and George
      Roy Elliott. New York: Longmans, Green, 1913,
      pp. 325-326.

174   "Leaves Motionless." English Essays. Ed. Walter
      Cochrane Bronson. New York: Holt, Rinehart and

Winston, 1905, pp. 257-259.

175   "Lichen. " Representative English Essays. Ed.
      Warner Taylor. New York: Harper, 1923, pp.
      404-405.

176   _____. Essays of the Past and Present. Ed.
      Warner Taylor. New York: Harper, 1927, pp.
      480-481.

177   _____. Types and Times in the Essay. Ed.
      Warner Taylor. New York: Harper, 1932, pp.
      78-79.

178   "Man's Best Wisdom. " Treasure Chest: An An-
      thology of Contemplative Prose. Ed. James
      Donald Adams. New York: E. P. Dutton, 1946,
      pp. 181-182.

179   "Mountain Glory. " English Prose: A Series of
      Related Essays for the Discussion of the Art of
      Writing. Ed. Frederick William Roe and George
      Roy Elliott. New York: Longmans, Green, 1913,
      pp. 328-332.

180   "Mountains. " English Essays. Ed. Walter Coch-
      rane Bronson. New York: Holt, Rinehart and
      Winston, 1905, pp. 256-257.

181   "Mystery of Life and Its Arts. " English and Engi-
      neering: A Volume of Essays for English Classes
      in Engineering Schools. Ed. Frank Aydelotte.
      New York: McGraw-Hill, 1923, pp. 377-409.

182   _____. Selected Nineteenth Century Essays.
      Ed. Clyde Kenneth Hyder and John Erskine Hankins.
      New York: Crofts, 1938, pp. 378-407.

183   "The Nature of Gothic. " The Nature of Art. Ed.
      John Gassner and Sidney Thomas. New York:
      Crown, 1964, pp. 227-259.

184   "Northland. " Representative English Essays. Ed.

Warner Taylor. New York: Harper, 1923, pp. 408-411.

185 _____. Essays of the Past and Present. Ed. Warner Taylor. New York: Harper, 1927, pp. 482-484.

186 "Of Kings' Treasuries. " Essays for College English. 2 vols. Ed. James Cloyd Bowman. Boston: D. C. Heath, 1915-1918, pp. 342-346.

187 _____. Essays and Studies: Prose Selections for College Reading. Ed. Frederick Miller Smith. Boston: Houghton Mifflin, 1922, pp. 3-32.

188 _____. Essaying the Essay. Ed. Burges Johnson. Boston: Little, Brown, 1927, pp. 223-238.

189 _____. Essays for College English. Ed. William Eugene Brennan. New York: Appleton-Century, 1930, pp. 236-259.

190 _____. Comparative Essays: Present and Past. Ed. Warren W. Read. New York: Noble and Noble, 1933, pp. 158-178. Reprinted: New York: Noble and Noble, 1948 and 1953.

191 _____. Prose and the Essay: A Developmental Anthology. Boston: Houghton Mifflin, 1962, pp. 270-277.

192 "Of the Pathetic Fallacy. " English Critical Essays. Ed. Edmund David Jones. London: Oxford University Press, 1916, pp. 378-397.

193 _____. Book of the Essay from Montaigne to E. B. White. Ed. Homer Carroll Combs. New York: Charles Scribner's Sons, 1950, pp. 289-302.

194 _____. English Literary Criticism: Romantic and Victorian. Ed. Daniel G. Hoffman and Samuel Lynn Hynes. New York: Appleton-Century-Crofts,

1963, pp. 201-217.

195   "Open Sky." Representative English Essays. Ed.
       Warner Taylor. New York: Harper, 1923, pp.
       405-408.

196   A Popular Handbook to the National Gallery Includ-
       ing, By Special Permission, Notes Collected from
       the Works of John Ruskin. Ed. Edward Tyas
       Cook. London: Macmillan, 1901.

197   "Relation of Art to Use." English, Science and
       Engineering: A Collection of Expository Essays
       for Students of Science and Engineering. Ed.
       Joshua Lawrence Eason and Maurice Harley We-
       seen. New York: Doubleday, Page, 1918, pp.
       316-329. Reprinted: New York: H. W. Wilson,
       circa 1974.

198   "Roots of Honor." College Life: Its Conditions
       and Problems: A Selection of Essays for Use in
       College Writing Courses. Ed. Maurice Garland
       Fulton. New York: Macmillan, 1914, pp. 483-
       499.

199   _____. The Victorian Mind: An Anthology.
       Ed. Gerald B. Kauvar and Gerald C. Sorensen.
       New York: G. P. Putnam's Sons, 1969, pp. 128-
       137.

200   "Running Water." English Essays. Ed. Walter
       Cochrane Bronson. New York: Holt, Rinehart and
       Winston, 1905, pp. 252-254.

201   Ruskin (and Others) on Byron. Ed. Raymond Wil-
       son Chambers. London: Oxford University Press,
       1925. (English Association Pamphlet No. 62.) Re
       printed: Philadelphia: Richard West, 1973. New
       York: Haskell House, 1970. (English Literature
       Series, No. 150.)

202   "St. Mark's Cathedral." Essays, English and
       American. Ed. Raymond MacDonald Alden. New

York: Charles Scribner's Sons, 1921, pp. 283-290.

203 _____. Harper's Anthology: Prose. Ed. F. A. Manchester and W. F. Giese. New York: Harper, 1926, pp. 715-721.

204 _____. Toward Today: A Collection of English and American Essays Presenting the Earlier Development of Ideas Fundamental in Modern Life and Literature. Ed. Erich Albert Walter. Chicago: Scott, Foresman, 1938, pp. 243-246.

205 "The Sea." English Essays. Ed. Walter Cochrane Bronson. New York: Holt, Rinehart and Winston, 1905, pp. 254-256.

206 "Sea-Painting." A Selection from the Best English Essays, Illustrative of the History of English Prose Style. Ed. Sherwin Cody. Chicago: A. G. McClurg, 1903, pp. 333-347.

207 "Sir Joshua and Holbein." Nineteenth Century Essays. Ed. George Sampson. London: Macmillan, 1912, pp. 130-140.

208 "The Sky." English Essays. Ed. Walter Cochrane Bronson. New York: Holt, Rinehart and Winston, 1905, pp. 250-252.

209 _____. Types of the Essay. Ed. Benjamin Alexander Heydrick. New York: Charles Scribner's Sons, 1921, pp. 105-111.

210 _____. Essays and Studies: Prose Selections for College Reading. Ed. Frederick Miller Smith. Boston: Houghton Mifflin, 1922, pp. 202-204.

211 _____. Century Readings in the English Essay. Ed. Louis Wann. New York: Appleton-Century, 1926, pp. 299-302.

212 _____. Prose Patterns. Ed. Arno Lehman

Bader, T. Hornberger, S. K. Proctor, and C. Wells. New York: Harcourt, Brace, 1933, pp. 477-479.

213   "Splendors of Sunset." English Prose: A Series of Related Essays for the Discussion of the Art of Writing. Ed. Frederick William Roe and George Roy Elliott. New York: Longmans, Green, 1913, pp. 333-334.

214   "Springs of Wandel." When I Was a Child: An Anthology. Ed. Edward Charles Wagenknecht. New York: E. P. Dutton, 1946, pp. 9-20.

215   "Traffic." Essays for College English. Ed. James Cloyd Bowman, Louis Ignacious Bredvold, Leroy Bethuel Greenfield, and Bruce Weirick. 2 vols. Boston: D. C. Heath, 1915-1918, vol. 1, 402-425.

216   _____. English and Engineering: A Volume of Essays for English Classes in Engineering Schools Ed. Frank Aydelotte. New York: McGraw-Hill, 1923, pp. 321-343.

217   _____. Adventures in Essay Reading. Michigan University Department of Rhetoric and Journalism. New York: Harcourt, Brace, 1924, pp. 137 162.

218   _____. Points of View for College Students. Ed. Paul Kaufman. New York: Doubleday, Doran 1926, pp. 193-221.
      The essay has been re-titled "How Architecture Expresses the Soul" in this book.

219   _____. Essays Old and New. Ed. Margaret M. Bryant. New York: Crofts, 1940, pp. 131-146.

220   "True Books." Treasure Chest: An Anthology of Contemplative Prose. Ed. James Donald Adams.

New York: E. P. Dutton, 1946, pp. 179-180.

221   "True Use of Wealth." Reading for Writing. Ed.
      Ivan Earle Taylor and Jay Saunders Redding. New
      York: Ronald Press, 1952, pp. 208-213.

222   "Two Boyhoods." Essays from Five Centuries.
      Ed. William Thomson Hastings and Kenneth Oliver
      Mason. Boston: Houghton Mifflin, 1929, pp. 274-
      285.

223   _____. Essays for Discussion. Ed. Anita P.
      Forbes. New York: Harper, 1931, pp. 279-293.
      Rev. ed. New York: Harper, 1940, pp. 391-405.

224   "Virtues of Architecture." A Selection from the
      Best English Essays, Illustrative of the History of
      English Prose Style. Ed. Sherwin Cody. Chicago:
      A. C. McClurg, 1903, pp. 347-360.

225   "Water." English Prose: A Series of Related Es-
      says for the Discussion of the Art of Writing. Ed.
      Frederick William Roe and George Roy Elliott.
      New York: Longmans, Green, 1913, pp. 327-328.

226   "What and How to Read." Types of the Essay.
      Ed. Benjamin Alexander Heydrick. New York:
      Charles Scribner's Sons, 1921, pp. 175-190.

227   _____. Nineteenth Century Essays from Cole-
      ridge to Pater. (Noble English, vol. 5.) Ed.
      David Brooks Cofer. New York: Thomas Nelson
      and Sons, 1929, pp. 136-153.

228   "White-Thorn Blossom." Essays, English and
      American. Ed. Raymond MacDonald Alden. New
      York: Charles Scribner's Sons, 1921, pp. 290-
      306.

229   _____. Representative English Essays. Ed.
      Warner Taylor. New York: Harper, 1923, pp.
      69-85.

230   "Work." Century Readings in the English Essay.
      Ed. Louis Wann. New York: Appleton-Century,
      1926, pp. 303-306.

231   "Work of Iron in Nature." Types of Prose Writ-
      ing. Ed. Clark Harris Slover and DeWitt Talmage
      Starnes. Boston: Houghton Mifflin, 1933, pp.
      54-61.

232   "Writing and Thinking." English and Engineering:
      A Volume of Essays for English Classes in Engi-
      neering Schools. Ed. Frank Aydelotte. New York:
      McGraw-Hill, 1923, pp. 1-3.

2.   Letters and Diaries

233   Ah, Sweet Lady. Ed. James S. Dearden. Bem-
      bridge: The Yellowsands Press, 1968.

234   The Best of Friends: Further Letters to Sydney
      Carlyle Cockerell. Ed. V. Meynell. London:
      Rupert Hart-Davis, 1956.
          See Friends of a Lifetime (entry no. 239).

235   The Brantwood Diary: With Selected and Related
      Letters and Sketches of Persons Mentioned. Ed.
      Helen Gill Viljoen. New Haven, Conn.: Yale Uni-
      versity Press, 1971.

236   The Contemptible Horse. Ed. N. H. Strouse.
      New York: Adagio Press, 1962.

237   Dearest Mama Talbot: A Selection of Letters Writ-
      ten by John Ruskin to Mrs. Fanny Talbot. Ed.
      Margaret E. Spence. London: George Allen and
      Unwin, 1966.

238   The Diaries of John Ruskin. 3 vols. Ed. Joan
      Evans and John Howard Whitehouse. London:

Clarendon Press, (Oxford), 1956, 1958, 1959.

239   Friends of a Lifetime: Letters to Sydney Carlyle
      Cockerell. Ed. V. Meynell. London: Cape,
      1940.
         See The Best of Friends, (entry no. 234).

240   The Froude-Ruskin Friendship as Represented
      Through Letters. Ed. Helen Gill Viljoen. New
      York: Pageant Press, 1966.

241   The Gulf of Years: Letters from John Ruskin to
      Kathleen Olander. Ed. Rayner Unwin. London:
      George Allen and Unwin, 1953.

242   An Ill-Assorted Marriage: An Unpublished Letter
      by John Ruskin. Ed. C. Shorter. London: pub-
      lished by the editor, 1915.

243   John Ruskin and Effie Gray: The Story of John
      Ruskin, Effie Gray and John Everett Millais, Told
      for the First Time in Their Unpublished Letters.
      Ed. William James. New York: Charles Scrib-
      ner's Sons, 1947. Reprinted without illustrations
      under the title The Order of Release (see entry no.
      254): London: Murray, 1948. Philadelphia:
      Richard West, 1973.

244   John Ruskin's Letters to Francesca and Memoirs
      of the Alexanders. Ed. Lucia Gray Swett. Boston:
      Lothrop, Lee and Shephard, 1931.

245   John Ruskin's Letters to William Ward: with a
      Short Biography of William Ward. Ed. William C.
      Ward and Alfred Mansfield Brookes. Boston:
      Marshall Jones, 1922 (reprint of 1892 edition).

246   Letters Addressed to Algernon Charles Swinburne
      by John Ruskin, William Morris, Sir Edward Burne-
      Jones and Dante Gabriel Rossetti. London: printed
      for private circulation by Thomas J. Wise, 1919.

247   Letters of John Ruskin to Bernard Quaritch, 1867-

1888. Ed. Charlotte Quaritch Wrentmore. London: Quaritch, 1939. Reprinted: Folcroft, Pa.:
Folcroft Library Editions, (1974).

248   Letters of John Ruskin to Charles Eliot Norton.
2 vols. Ed. Charles Eliot Norton. Boston:
Houghton Mifflin, 1905.

249   The Letters of John Ruskin to Lord and Lady
Mount-Temple. Ed. John Lewis Bradley. Columbus, Ohio: Ohio State University Press, 1964.

250   Letters to M. G. and H. G. Edinburgh: privately
printed, 1903.
         "M. G. and H. G." are Mary Gladstone and
         Helen Gladstone.

251   The Library Edition of the Works of John Ruskin.
39 vols. Ed. Edward Tyas Cook and Alexander
Wedderburn. London: George Allen, 1903-1912.
         Letters are in volumes 16, 36 and 37. See
         also The Works of John Ruskin (entry no. 261).

252   Life of Octavia Hill. Ed. C. E. Maurice. London: Macmillan, 1913.
         Contains letters by John Ruskin.

253   Octavia Hill: Early Ideals. Ed. E. S. Maurice.
London: George Allen and Unwin, 1928.
         Contains letters by John Ruskin.

254   The Order of Release: The Story of John Ruskin,
Effie Gray and John Everett Millais Told for the
First Time in Their Unpublished Letters. Ed.
William James. London: Murray, 1948.
         This is a reprinting of John Ruskin and Effie
         Gray (see entry no. 243) using the same pagina-
         tion but sans illustrations. Reprint of 1948 edi-
         tion: Philadelphia: Richard West, 1973.

255   The Ruskin Family Letters: The Correspondence
of John James Ruskin, His Wife, and Their Son,
John, 1801-1843. 2 vols. Vol. I, 1801-1837, and

Vol. II, 1837-1843. Ed. Van Akin Burd. Ithaca, New York: Cornel University Press, 1973.

256 Ruskin in Italy: Letters to His Parents, 1845. Ed. Harold Shapiro. New York: Oxford University Press, 1972.

257 Ruskin's Letters from Venice, 1851-1852. Ed. J. L. Bradley. New Haven, Conn.: Yale University Press, 1955. (Yale Studies in English, vol. 129.) London: Oxford University Press, 1956.

258 The Solitary Warrior: New Letters by Ruskin. Ed. John Howard Whitehouse. London: George Allen and Unwin, 1929. Boston: Houghton Mifflin, 1930.

259 Sublime and Instructive: Letters from John Ruskin to Louisa, Marchioness of Waterford, Anna Blunden and Ellen Heaton. Ed. Virginia Surtees. London: M. Joseph, 1972.

260 The Winnington Letters: John Ruskin's Correspondence with Margaret Alexis Bell and the Children at Winnington Hall. Ed. Van Akin Burd. London: George Allen and Unwin, 1969. Cambridge, Mass.: Harvard University Press, 1970.

261 The Works of John Ruskin. 39 vols. Ed. Edward Tyas Cook and Alexander Wedderburn. New York: Longmans, Green, 1903-1912.
    Letters are in volumes 16, 36 and 37. See also The Library Edition of the Works of John Ruskin, (entry no. 251).

B. CRITICISM AND SCHOLARSHIP

1. Books Devoted Solely or in Substance to Ruskin

262 Alexander, Edward. Matthew Arnold, John Ruskin and the Modern Temper. Columbus, Ohio: Ohio State University Press, 1973.

263 Arts Council of Aldeburgh, London, and Colchester. Drawings by John Ruskin. London: Arts Council, 1960.

264 Arts Council of Great Britain. Ruskin and His Circle. London: Arts Council Gallery, 1964.

265 Ashbee, C. R. An Endeavor Towards the Teaching of John Ruskin and William Morris. London: Arnold, 1901. Reprinted: Philadelphia: Richard West, 1973. Reprinted: Folcroft, Pa.: Folcroft Library Editions, (1974).

266 Atkinson, B. Ruskin's Social Experiment at Barmouth. London: James Clarke, (1900).

267 Autret, Jean. Ruskin and the French Before Marcel Proust (With the Collected Fragmentary Translations). Genève: Droz, 1965.
Jean Autret has also published work on John Ruskin in French.

268 Axon, William E. A. John Ruskin: A Bibliographical Biography. Ann Arbor, Mich.: University Microfilms, 1965 (Xerox reprint of 1879 edition). Folcroft, Pa.: Folcroft Library Editions,

(1974) (reprint of 1879 edition). New York: Gordon Press, (1974).
The 1879 edition was volume 6 of the Papers of the Manchester Literary Club.

269 Bell, Quentin. Ruskin. Edinburgh: Oliver and Boyd, 1963.

270 Bembridge School, Isle of Wight. The Ruskin Gallery, Being Part of the Collection Made by John Howard Whitehouse, Esq., and Consisting Mainly of Drawings by John Ruskin. Isle of Wight: Bembridge School, no date.

271 Benson, Arthur Christopher. Ruskin: A Study in Personality. New York: G. P. Putnam's Sons, 1911. London: Smith, Elder, 1911. Philadelphia: Richard West, 1973. Folcroft, Pa.: Folcroft Library Editions, 1974. New York: Gordon Press, (1974). Saint Clair Shores, Mich.: Scholarly Press, (1974).

272 Bradley, John L. An Introduction to Ruskin. Boston: Houghton Mifflin, 1971.

273 Browning, Robert. Letter from Robert Browning to John Ruskin. Waco, Texas: Armstrong Browning Library, Baylor University, 1958. (Baylor University Baylor Browning Interests, number 17.)

274 Burdon, J. Reminiscences of Ruskin, by a St. George's Companion. London: 1919.

275 Burgess, W. Religion of Ruskin. Old Tappan, N.J.: H. Revell, 1906.

276 Carlyle, Thomas. Carlyle's Letters to Ruskin: A Finding List with Some Unpublished Letters. Ed. Charles Richard Sanders. Manchester: The John Rylands Library and the Manchester University Press, 1958.

277 Carter, J. and Pollard, G. An Enquiry into the

Nature of Certain Nineteenth-Century Pamphlets.
London: Constable, 1934.
    This book discusses Thomas Wise's forgeries
    of pamphlets he claimed were written by John
    Ruskin.

278   Chevrillon, André Louis. Philosophy of Ruskin.
New York: E. P. Dutton, 1914.
    André Chevrillon has also published work on
    John Ruskin in French.

279   City Art Gallery. Ruskin. Manchester: City Art
Gallery, 1904.

280   Clark, Kenneth. Ruskin at Oxford: An Inaugural
Lecture Delivered Before the University of Oxford,
14 November 1946. London: The Clarendon
Press (Oxford University Press), 1947.

281   _____. Drawings by John Ruskin. London:
Arts Council, 1960.

282   _____. Ruskin: An Anthology. New York:
Roy, (1974).

283   Collingwood, William Gersham. The Art of Teaching of John Ruskin. London: Rivingtons, 1900.

284   _____. The Life of John Ruskin. London:
Methuen, 1900 (rev. ed., 1905). Boston: Houghton
Mifflin: 1900. Reprinted: Philadelphia: Richard
West, 1973. New York: Haskell House, 1974.
(John Ruskin Series, number 87.)

285   _____. The Life and Work of John Ruskin.
London: Methuen, rev. ed., 1900. (First edition:
1893.)

286   _____. Ruskin As Artist. London: Royal Society of Painters in Water Colours, 1901.

287   _____. The Ruskin Cross at Coniston Described
and Illustrated. Ulverston: W. Holmes, 1901.

288   _____. Ruskin Relics. London: Isbister, 1903.
Reprinted: Philadelphia: Richard West, 1973.

289   _____. Catalogue of the Ruskin Exhibition.
Manchester: City Art Gallery, 1904.

290   _____. Ruskin's Philosophy. Coniston: Ken-
dall Titus Wilson and Son, 1922. Reprinted: Chi-
chester: Quentin Nelson, 1971.
A lecture given at the Ruskin Centenary Confer-
ence, Coniston, August 18, 1919.

291   _____. The Art Teaching of John Ruskin.
Philadelphia: Richard West, 1973 (reprint of 1891
edition).

292   Coniston Institute. Ruskin Museum Catalogue.
5th edition. Coniston Institute, 1919.

293   Cook, Edward Tyas. The Life of John Ruskin. 2
vols. (vol. one: 1819-1860, and vol. two: 1860-
1900). London: George Allen, 1911. New York:
Macmillan, 1911. Reprinted: 2 vols. New York:
Haskell House, 1968. (English Biography Series,
number 31.) Reprinted: 2 vols. Philadelphia:
Richard West, 1973.

294   _____. Homes and Haunts of John Ruskin. New
York: Macmillan, 1912. Reprinted: Philadelphia:
Richard West, 1973.

295   _____. Studies in Ruskin: Some Aspects of the
Work and Teaching of John Ruskin. Philadelphia:
Richard West, 1973 (reprint of 1890 edition). Port
Washington, N.Y.: Kennikat Press, 1972. Folk-
stone, Kent, England: Bailey Brothers and Swinfen,
1972.

296   Crow, Gerald H. Ruskin. London: Duckworth,
1936.

297   Curtin, Frank Daniel. Aesthetics in English Social
Reform. Chicago: University of Chicago Libraries,
1940.

See also Curtin, Frank Daniel. "Aesthetics in English Social Reform: Ruskin and His Followers," entry no. 441.

298   Davison, E. Ruskin and His Circle. London: The Arts Council, 1964.

299   Dearden, James S. Catalogue of the Pictures by John Ruskin and Other Artists at Brantwood, Coniston. Isle of Wight: The Education Trust, 1960.

300   _____ . Ruskin Association Books. Bembridge: The Yellowsands Press, 1962.

301   _____ , ed. The Professor: Arthur Severn's Memoir of John Ruskin. London: George Allen and Unwin, 1967.

302   _____ . Brantwood: Books from John Ruskin's Library. Bembridge: The Yellowsands Press, 1967.

303   _____ . Catalogue of the Drawings by John Ruskin on Permanent Exhibition in the Ruskin Gallery, Bembridge School. Bembridge: The Yellowsands Press, 1967.

304   _____ . Facets of Ruskin: Some Sesquicentennial Studies. London: Charles Skilton, 1970.

305   _____ . Ruskin and Coniston. London: Covent Garden Press, 1971.

306   _____ . John Ruskin. New York: International Publications Service, 1973. (Lifelines Series, number 15.)

307   _____ . John Ruskin: An Illustrated Life of John Ruskin, 1819-1900. London: Shire, 1973.

308   _____ . Ruskin. Boston: Newbury Books, (1974).

309   de La Sizeranne, R. Ruskin at Venice. London:
      George Allen, 1906.
          The author has also published works on John
      Ruskin in French.

310   Dolk, Lester Charles. The Aesthetics of John
      Ruskin in Relation to the Aesthetics of the Roman-
      tic Era. Urbana, Ill.: University of Illinois, 1941.

311   Downes, Robert Percival. John Ruskin: A Study.
      Folcroft, Pa.: Folcroft Library Editions, 1973
      (originally published in 1890).

312   Drummond, J., Monfries, C., and Hollingworth,
      G. E. Unto This Last. London: University Tu-
      torial Press, 1931.

313   Earland, Ada. Ruskin and His Circle. London:
      Hutchinson, 1910. Reprinted: New York: AMS
      Press, 1971. Reprinted: Philadelphia: Richard
      West, 1973.

314   Evans, Joan. John Ruskin. London: Oxford Uni-
      versity Press, 1954. Reprinted: New York:
      Haskell House, 1970. (English Biography Series,
      number 31.)

315   Fain, John Tyree. Ruskin and the Economists.
      Nashville, Tenn.: Vanderbilt University Press,
      1956.

316   Farrar, Frederic William. Ruskin as a Religious
      Teacher. Folcroft, Pa.: Folcroft Library Edi-
      tions, 1973 (originally published in 1904).

317   Fogg Art Museum. Ruskin, In Memory of Charles
      Eliot Norton. Cambridge, Mass.: Harvard Uni-
      versity Press, 1909-1910.

318   _____. Paintings and Drawings of the Pre-
      Raphaelites and Their Circle. Cambridge, Mass.:
      Harvard University Press, 1946.

319   Garrigan, Kristine Ottesen. Ruskin on Architec-
       ture: His Thought and Influence. Madison, Wis.:
       University of Wisconsin Press, 1973.

320   Geddes, Patrick. John Ruskin: Economist. Fol-
       croft, Pa.: Folcroft Library Editions, 1973 (re-
       print of 1884 edition).

321   George Allen. List. London: George Allen, 1900.
       This is a list of works by John Ruskin.

322   Gibbs, Ellen and Gibbs, Mary. The Bible Refer-
       ences of John Ruskin. New York: Gordon Press,
       (1974).

323   Goetz, Mary Dorothea. A Study of Ruskin's Con-
       cept of the Imagination. Washington, D.C.: The
       Catholic University of America, 1947.

324   Goodspeed's Book Shop. A Catalogue of Paintings,
       Drawings and Manuscripts by John Ruskin: To
       Which Is Added a Description of Ruskin's Celestial
       Globe, and of a Few Books from His Library at
       Brantwood. Boston: Goodspeed's Book Shop, 1932.

325   Graham, J. W. The Harvest of Ruskin. London:
       George Allen, 1920. Reprinted: Philadelphia:
       Richard West, 1973.

326   Hagstotz, Hilda Boettcher. The Educational The-
       ories of John Ruskin. · Lincoln, Neb.: University
       of Nebraska Press, 1942.

327   Harrison, Frederic H. John Ruskin. London:
       Macmillan, 1902 (reprinted in 1907 and 1925). Re-
       printed: Detroit, Mich.: Gale Research, 1971.
       New York: Gryphon Books, 1971. Folcroft, Pa.:
       Folcroft Library Editions, 1973.

328   Herrmann, Luke. Ruskin and Turner: A Study of
       Ruskin As a Collector of Turner, Based on His
       Gifts to the University of Oxford: Incorporating a
       Catalogue Raisonné of the Turner Drawings in the

Ashmolean Museum. London: Faber and Faber,
1968. New York: Frederic A. Praeger, 1969.

329   Hobson, John Atkinson. John Ruskin: Social Re-
former. New York: Gordon Press, (1974).
(First published in 1898.)
See also entry no. 330.

330   _____. John Ruskin As a Social Reformer.
Philadelphia: Richard West, 1973 (reprint of 1899
edition).

331   Jameson, Mary Ethel, ed. A Bibliographical Con-
tribution to the Study of John Ruskin. Cambridge:
Riverside Press, 1901. Reprinted: Folcroft,
Pa.: Folcroft Library Editions, 1973.

332   Kitchin, G. W. Ruskin in Oxford and Other
Studies. London: Murray, 1904. Reprinted:
Philadelphia: Richard West, 1973.

333   Ladd, Henry Andrews. The Victorian Morality of
Art: An Analysis of Ruskin's Esthetic. New York:
Ray Long and Richard R. Smith, 1932. New York:
Octagon Books, 1968.

334   Lakshmi Menon, V. Ruskin and Gandhi. Sarva
Seva Sangh Prakashan, 1965.

335   Landow, George P. The Aesthetic and Critical
Theories of John Ruskin. Princeton, N. J.:
Princeton University Press, 1971.

336   Larg, David. John Ruskin. London: Peter
Davies, 1932 (also 1935). New York: D. Appleton, 1933. New York: Thomas Nelson and Sons,
1939. Reprint of Appleton edition: Philadelphia:
Richard West, 1973. New York: Haskell House,
1974. (John Ruskin Series, number 87.) Folcroft,
Pa.: Folcroft Library Editions, 1974.

337   Leon, Derrick. Ruskin: The Great Victorian.
London: Routledge and Kegan Paul, 1949 (reprinted

in 1969). Reprinted: Hamden, Conn.: Shoe
String Press, 1969. Reprinted: Philadelphia:
Richard West, (1974).

338 Links, J. G. The Ruskins in Normandy: A Tour
     in 1848 with Murray's Handbook. London: Murray,
     1968. New York: Vanguard Press, 1974.

339 Livingstone, R. W. Ruskin. London: Oxford
     University Press, 1945. Folcroft, Pa.: Folcroft
     University Press, 1945.
        This was a Hertz Lecture given at the British
        Academy.

340 Lutyens, Mary. Millais and the Ruskins. London:
     Murray, 1967. New York: Vanguard Press, 1968.

341 _____. The Ruskins and the Grays. London:
     J. Murray, 1972. New York: Vanguard Press,
     1974.

342 McLaughlin, Elizabeth T. Ruskin and Gandhi.
     Lewisburg, Pa.: Bucknell University Press, 1973.
     London: Associated University Presses, 1974.

343 Mallock, W. H. The New Republic: Ruskin Is
     Described as Mr. Herbert. Philadelphia: Richard
     West, (1974).

344 Masefield, J. John Ruskin. Bembridge: The
     Yellowsands Press, 1920.

345 Mather, J. Marshall. John Ruskin: His Life and
     Teaching. New York: Haskell House, 1972 (re-
     print of 1903 edition). (English Biography Series,
     number 31.) Philadelphia: Richard West, 1973
     (reprint of 1883 edition). Folcroft, Pa.: Folcroft
     Library Editions, (1974) (reprint of 1903 edition).
        The second edition of this book was published in
        1884 under the title: Life and Teaching of John
        Ruskin. A revised edition was published in
        1890.

346 Meynell, Alice Christiana Thompson. John Ruskin. New York: Dodd, Mead, 1900. Edinburgh: Blackwood and Son, 1900. Reprinted: Folcroft, Pa. : Folcroft Library Editions, 1972.

347 Miller, A. Ruskin Re-considered. London: The Art Workers' Guild, 1929.

348 Montgomery, J. S. John Ruskin: The Voice of the New Age. New York: Methodist Book Concern, 1902. Reprinted: Folcroft, Pa. : Folcroft Library Editions, (1974).

349 Morley, Edith J. John Ruskin and Social Ethics. London: Fabian Trace and Edition, 1926. Folcroft, Pa. : Folcroft Library Editions, 1928.

350 O'Brien, Mary Corita. The Personalist Element in the Sociological Ideas of John Ruskin. Washington, D. C. : The Catholic University of America, 1939.

351 Pearson, Peter Henry. Ruskin -- Sesame and Lilies: Questions for Interpretative and Literary Study. Lindsburg, Kan. : P. H. Pearson, 1914.

352 Pengelly, R. E. John Ruskin; A Biographical Sketch. London: Melrose, no date.

353 Pevsner, Nikolaus. Ruskin and Viollet-le-Duc: Englishness and Frenchness in the Appreciation of Gothic Architecture. London: Thames and Hudson, 1969.

354 Powell, F. York. John Ruskin and Thought on Democracy. London: The St. George Library Series, 1905.

355 Proust, Marcel. Days of Pilgrimage: Ruskin at Notre-Dame d'Amiens, and John Ruskin. G. Hopkins, trans. London: 1948.
Marcel Proust also published works on John Ruskin in French.

356   Queens College of the City of New York.   Ruskin's
      Backgrounds, Friendships, and Interests As Re-
      flected in the F. J. Sharp Collection Loaned by
      Helen Gill Viljoen.   Flushing, New York: Paul
      Klapper Library, 1965.
      Exhibition January-February 1965.

357   Quennell, Peter.   John Ruskin: The Portrait of a
      Prophet.   London: Collins, 1949.   Reprinted:
      Philadelphia: Richard West, 1973.

358   _____.   John Ruskin.   New York: Longmans,
      Green, 1956.   (Writers and Their Work, number
      76.)   New York: British Book Center, (1974).
      New York: Haskell House, 1974.   (John Ruskin
      Series, number 87.)

359   Ratchford, F. E., ed.   Between the Lines: Let-
      ters and Memoranda Interchanged by H. Buxton
      Forman and Thomas J. Wise.   Austin, Texas:
      University of Texas Press, 1945.

360   Rawnsley, H. D.   Ruskin and the English Lakes.
      Glasgow: Maclehose, 1901.   Reprinted: Philadel-
      phia: Richard West, 1973.

361   Roe, Frederick William.   The Social Philosophy of
      Carlyle and Ruskin.   New York: Harcourt Brace,
      1921.   Reprinted: New York: Peter Smith, 1936.
      Reprinted: Port Washington, N.Y.:   Kennikat
      Press, 1969.   Reprinted: Staten Island, N.Y.:
      Gordian Press, 1970.

362   Rosenberg, John D.   The Darkening Glass: A
      Portrait of Ruskin's Genius.   New York: Columbia
      University Press, 1961.   London: Routledge and
      Kegan Paul, 1963.

363   Rossetti, William Michael, ed.   Ruskin: Rossetti:
      PreRaphaelitism: Papers 1854 to 1862.   New York:
      AMS Press, 1971 (reprint of 1899 edition).   Fol-
      croft, Pa.:   Folcroft Library Editions, 1973.

364 Sanders, Charles Richard. Carlyle's Letters to
     Ruskin: A Finding List with Some Unpublished
     Letters. Manchester: The John Rylands Library
     and the Manchester University Press, 1958.

365 Schumacher, Charles Augustus. John Ruskin.
     Oneonta, N. Y.: the author, 1929.

366 Scott, E. R. Ruskin's Guild of St. George. Lon-
     don: Methuen, 1931.

367 Scudder, V. D. Introduction to the Writings of
     John Ruskin. Philadelphia: Richard West, 1973
     (reprint of 1890 edition).

368 Shaw, George Bernard. Ruskin's Politics. Lon-
     don: The Ruskin Centenary Council, 1921. Fol-
     croft, Pa.: Folcroft Library Editions, (1974).
        A lecture delivered at the Royal Academy, No-
        vember 21, 1919.

369 Shaw, W. H. John Ruskin: Ethical and Religious
     Teacher. London: Oxford University Press, 1901.

370 Shepherd, Richard H. Bibliography of Ruskin.
     Folcroft, Pa.: Folcroft Library Editions, (1974)
     (reprint of 1879 edition).

371 Sherburne, James Clark. John Ruskin: Or, The
     Ambiguities of Abundance: A Study in Social and
     Economic Criticism. Cambridge, Mass.: Harvard
     University Press, 1972.

372 Skelton, Robin, ed. John Ruskin: The Final Years.
     London: 1955.

373 Skilton, Charles. The Paintings and Drawings of
     John Ruskin, Hon. R. W. S. London: The Old
     Watercolour Society, 1969. (44th annual volume.)

374 Smart, William A. A Disciple of Plato: A Criti-
     cal Study of John Ruskin. Folcroft, Pa.: Folcroft
     Library Editions, 1974 (reprint of 1883 edition).

375   . John Ruskin: His Life and Work. Folcroft, Pa. : Folcroft Library Editions, 1973 (original edition published in 1880).

376   Sotheby and Co. Catalogue of the Collection of
Pictures and Drawings Formerly the Property of
John Ruskin. May 20, 1931.

377   . Catalogue of Old English Silver, the
Property of the Late Professor John Ruskin, Re-
moved from Brantwood, Coniston, and the Property of the Late Joseph Arthur Severn. April 29,
1931.

378   Spielmann, Marion Harry. John Ruskin: A Sketch
of His Life, His Work, and His Opinions, with
Personal Reminiscences, Together with a Paper by
John Ruskin, Entitled "The Black Arts." New
York: Cassell, 1900. Reprinted: Folcroft, Pa. :
Folcroft Library Editions, 1974.

379   Statham, Henry Heathcote. The Truth About Ruskin. New York: Tucker Publishing Co. , 1900.

380   Stein, Roger Breed. John Ruskin and Aesthetic
Thought in America, 1840-1900. Cambridge,
Mass. : Harvard University Press, 1967.

381   Symon, James D. John Ruskin: His Homes and
Haunts. Philadelphia: Richard West, 1973.

382   Symon, James David and Bensusan, Samuel Levy.
John Ruskin. New York: Dodge, 1912.

383   Townsend, Francis G. Ruskin and the Landscape
Feeling: A Critical Analysis of His Thought During
the Crucial Years of His Life, 1843-1856. Urbana:
University of Illinois Press, 1951. (Illinois Studies
in Language and Literature, 35 [1951].)

384   Verst, E. B. The Socialism of Ruskin and Morris.
Chicago: University of Illinois, 1956.

385   Viljoen, Helen Gill. Ruskin's Scottish Heritage:
       A Prelude. Urbana: University of Illinois Press,
       1956.

386   _____. Ruskin's Backgrounds, Friendships and
       Interests. New York: Queen's College Library,
       1965. (Exhibition catalogue.)

387   Waldstein, Charles. The Work of John Ruskin:
       Its Influence Upon Modern Thought and Life. Phil-
       adelphia: Richard West, 1973 (reprint of 1894 edi-
       tion).

388   Walton, Paul H. The Drawings of John Ruskin.
       Oxford: Clarendon Press, 1972.

389   Webling, P. A Sketch of John Ruskin. London:
       published by the author, (1914).

390   Whitehouse, John Howard, ed. Ruskin Centenary
       Addresses, 8 February 1919. London: Oxford
       University Press, 1919.
            Addresses: O. M. Bryce, John William Mac-
            kail, Henry Wilson, Edward Tyas Cook, and
            Alexander Wedderburn. Communication: Her-
            bert Warren. Essay: John Howard Whitehouse.

391   _____, ed. John Ruskin: Letters Written On
       the Occasion of the Centenary of His Birth 1919.
       London: Oxford University Press (for the Ruskin
       Centenary Council), 1919.

392   _____, ed. Ruskin the Prophet and Other Cen-
       tenary Studies. New York: E. P. Dutton, 1920.
       Folcroft, Pa.: Folcroft Library Editions, 1973.

393   _____. John Ruskin. London: Ivor Nicholson
       and Watson, 1934.

394   _____, ed. To the Memory of Ruskin. Cam-
       bridge, Eng.: Cambridge University Press (for
       the Ruskin Society), 1934. Folcroft, Pa.: Fol-
       croft Library Editions, (1974).

395   . Ruskin and Brantwood: An Account of
the Exhibition Rooms. Cambridge, Eng.: Cambridge University Press (for the Ruskin Society),
1937. Folcroft, Pa.: Folcroft Library Editions,
(1974).

396   , ed. Poems to Ruskin. Oxford:
Friends of Brantwood Society and the Ruskin Society, 1941.

397   , ed. Ruskin's Influence Today. London:
Oxford University Press (for the Ruskin Society),
1945. Folcroft, Pa.: Folcroft Library Editions,
1974.

398   , ed. Ruskin: Renascence. London:
Oxford University Press (for the Ruskin Society),
1946.

399   , ed. Ruskin: Prophet of the Good Life.
London: Oxford University Press, 1948. Folcroft,
Pa.: Folcroft Library Editions, (1974).

400   . Vindication of Ruskin. London: George
Allen and Unwin, 1950. Reprinted: Philadelphia:
Richard West, (1974).
       Whitehouse wrote this work as a reply to The
       Order of Release by Admiral William James.

401   . John Ruskin. London: Oxford University Press (for the Ruskin Society), 1953. New
York: Haskell House, 1974. (John Ruskin Series,
number 87.)

402   Wilenski, Reginald Howard. John Ruskin: An In-
troduction to Further Study of His Life and Work.
London: Faber and Faber, 1933. Reprinted:
New York: Russell and Russell, 1967. Reprinted:
Philadelphia: Richard West, 1973. Folcroft, Pa.:
Folcroft Library Editions, (1974).

403   Williams-Ellis, Amabel. The Tragedy of John
Ruskin. London: Cape, 1928. Reprinted: Phila-

delphia: Richard West, 1973.
The second edition of this work was printed as
follows: The Exquisite Tragedy: An Intimate
Life of John Ruskin. Garden City, N.Y. :
Doubleday, Doran, 1929. Reprinted: Philadel-
phia: Richard West, 1973.
The third edition of this work was printed as
follows: John Ruskin. London: J. Cape, 1933.
(Life and Letters Series, number 52.)

404   Wingate, Ashmore. Life of John Ruskin. London:
Walter Scott, 1910.   Folcroft, Pa. : Folcroft Library Editions, (1974).

405   Wise, Thomas James and Smart, James P. , comp.
A Complete Bibliography of the Writings in Prose
and Verse of John Ruskin LL. D. With a List of
the More Important Ruskiniana.   2 vols.   London:
Dawsons of Pall Mall, 1964 (reprint of 1893 edition).   Atlantic Highlands, N. J. : Fernhill House,
1964.
Due to complications created by the Wise for-
geries, care is necessary when utilizing this
work as a reference.

406   Woodall, James R. Ruskin and the Rose. Nash-
ville, Tenn. : 1952.
Summary of a Vanderbilt University dissertation.

407   Yount, C. A. The Reaction Against Ruskin in Art
Criticism, Art and Morality. Chicago: University
of Chicago Libraries, 1941.

2.   Inclusions in works not devoted solely to Ruskin

408   Alexander, Edward. "Roles of the Victorian Critic:
Matthew Arnold and John Ruskin. " Literary Criticism and Historical Understanding: Selected Papers
from the English Institute. Ed. Philip W. Damon.

New York: Columbia University Press, 1966, pp.
53-84.

409   Angeli, H. R.   Dante Gabriel Rossetti, His
      Friends and Enemies.   London: Hamish Hamilton,
      1949.

410   Atlay, J. B.   Sir Henry Wentworth Acland, a
      Memoir.   London: Smith, Elder, 1903.

411   Avebury, John Lubbock.   "John Ruskin."   Essays
      and Addresses, 1900-1903.   London: Macmillan,
      1903, pp. 44-66.

412   Ball, Patricia M.   The Science of Aspects: The
      Changing Role of Fact in the Work of Coleridge,
      Ruskin and Hopkins.   London: Athlone Press,
      1971.

413   Bartlett, Mabel and Baker, Sophia.   Mothers--
      Makers of Men.   2nd rev. ed.   New York: Expo-
      sition, 1952, pp. 70-74.

414   Beard, Charles Austin.   "Ruskin and the Babble of
      Tongues."   College Book of Essays.   Ed. John
      Abbot Clark.   New York: Holt, 1939, pp. 653-659.

415   Beardsley, Monroe Curtis.   "The Artist and Socie-
      ty."   Aesthetics from Classical Greece to the Pres-
      ent: A Short History.   New York: Macmillan,
      1966, pp. 283-316.

416   Bell, E. Moberly.   Octavia Hill.   London: Con-
      stable, 1942.

417   Benét, Laura.   Famous Storytellers for Young Peo-
      ple.   New York: Dodd, 1968, pp. 41-46.

418   Benson, Arthur Christopher.   "A Sight of Ruskin."
      Memories and Friends.   New York and London:
      G. P. Putnam's Sons, 1924, pp. 20-31.

419   Birkenhead, S.   Illustrious Friends: The Story of

Joseph Severn and His Son Arthur.   London:
Hamish Hamilton, 1965.

420   Blunt, W. Cockerell: Sydney Carlyle Cockerell,
      Friend of Ruskin and William Morris and Director
      of the Fitzwilliam Museum, Cambridge.   London:
      Hamish Hamilton, 1964.

421   Bottrall, Margaret Florence Saumarez. Personal
      Records. London: Rupert Hart-Davis, 1961, pp.
      30-33, 230.

422   Briggs, Martin S. "John Ruskin and William Mor-
      ris." Men of Taste. London: Batsford, 1947.

423   Brooks, Van Wyck. Dream of Arcadia. New York:
      E. P. Dutton, 1958, pp. 73-76, 122-124, 176-188.

424   Brownell, William Crary. "Ruskin." Victorian
      Prose Masters. New York: Scribner, 1901, pp.
      205-230.

425   Buckley, J. H. "The Moral Aesthetic." The Vic-
      torian Temper: A Study in Literary Culture. Cam-
      bridge, Mass. : Harvard University Press, 1951.

426   Burne-Jones, G. Memorials of Edward Burne-
      Jones. 2 vols. London: Macmillan, 1904.

427   Butler, Dugald. "John Ruskin's Grandfather, a
      Merchant at the West of the Tron Kirk." The
      Tron Kirk of Edinburgh: Or Christ's Kirk at the
      Tron: A History. Edinburgh: Oliphant, Anderson
      and Ferrier, 1906 chapter 13.

428   Chambers, Raymond Wilson. "Ruskin (and Others)
      on Byron." Man's Unconquerable Mind: Studies of
      English Writers from Bede to A. E. Housman and
      W. P. Ker. Toronto: Nelson, 1939, pp. 311-341.

429   Chandler, Alice. "Art and Society: Ruskin and
      Morris." A Dream of Order: Medieval Ideal in
      Nineteenth-Century England. Lincoln, Neb. :

University of Nebraska Press, 1970, pp. 184-230.

430   Chapman, Raymond. "Ruskin." The Victorian
       Debate: English Literature and Society, 1832-1901.
       New York: Basic Books, 1968, pp. 207-216.

431   Chesterton, Gilbert Keith. "Ruskin." Varied
       Types. New York: Dodd, 1903, pp. 217-222.

432   _____. "John Ruskin." Handful of Authors:
       Essays on Books and Writers. Ed. Dorothy Col-
       lins. London: Sheed, 1953, pp. 147-156.

433   Chrisman, Lewis Herbert. "John Ruskin, Preach-
       er." John Ruskin, Preacher, and Other Essays.
       New York: Abingdon Press, 1921, pp. 7-24.

434   Chubb, Edwin Watts. "Ruskin." Masters of Eng-
       lish Literature. Chicago: A. C. McClurg, 1914,
       pp. 379-397.

435   _____. "Ruskin's Childhood." Stories of Au-
       thors, British and American. London: Macmillan,
       1926, pp. 130-134.

436   Collingwood, Robin George. "Ruskin's Philosophy."
       Essays in the Philosophy of Art. Ed. Alan Dona-
       gan. Bloomington, Ind.: Indiana University Press,
       1964, pp. 3-41.

437   Colvin, Sidney. "John Ruskin." Memories and
       Notes of Persons and Places, 1852-1912. London:
       Arnold, 1921, pp. 38-47.

438   Cook, Edward Tyas. "Some Remarks on Ruskin's
       Style." Literary Recreations. London: Macmil-
       lan, 1918, pp. 34-54.
       Ruskin is also quoted throughout this book.

439   Cooke, George Willis. "Ruskin." Poets and Prob-
       lems. Folcroft, Pa.: Folcroft Library Editions,
       1972 (reprint of 1886 edition), pp. 171-267.

440 Cunliffe, John William. "Early Victorian Prose
Writers." Leaders of the Victorian Revolution.
New York: Appleton-Century, 1934, pp. 35-71.

441 Curtin, Frank Daniel. "Aesthetics in English Social Reform: Ruskin and His Followers." Nineteenth Century Studies. Ed. Herbert Davies, William C. DeVaue, and R. C. Bald. Ithaca, N.Y.:
Cornell University Press, 1940, pp. 199-245.
     See also Curtin, Frank Daniel. Aesthetics in
English Social Reform, entry no. 297.

442 Davies, J. Llewellyn. The Working Men's College,
1854-1904. London: 1904.

443 Dougherty, Charles Thomas. "Of Ruskin's Gar-
dens." Myth and Symbol: Critical Approaches and
Applications. Ed. Bernice Slote. Lincoln, Neb.:
University of Nebraska Press, 1963, pp. 141-151.
     Dougherty discusses Modern Painters V and
"Sesame and Lilies."

444 Doughty, Oswald. "Ruskin." A Victorian Romantic: Dante Gabriel Rossetti. 2nd ed. rev., 1960.
London: Oxford University Press, 1949, pp. 157-
179.
     Doughty makes numerous references to Ruskin
throughout this book.

445 Doyle, Brian, ed. Who's Who of Children's Literature. New York: Schocken, 1968, pp. 235-236.

446 Drew, Mary Gladstone. "Mr. Ruskin and Rose."
Acton, Gladstone and Others. London: Nisbet,
1924, pp. 104-118.

447 Dunn, Waldo Hilary. "Ruskin and the Values of
Life." Lectures on Three Eminent Victorians.
Claremont, Calif.: Scripps College, 1933.

448 Ellman, Richard. "Overtures to 'Salome.'" Golden
Codgers: Biographical Speculations. New York:
Oxford University Press, 1973, pp. 39-59.

449   Ernest, E. , ed. The Kate Greenaway Treasury.
      London: Collins, 1968.

450   Feiling, Keith. In Christ Church Hall. New York:
      Macmillan, 1960, pp. 173-185.

451   Finberg, Alexander Joseph. The Life of J. M. W.
      Turner, R. A. London: Clarendon Press (Oxford),
      1939. Second edition. Revised by Hilda F. Fin-
      berg. London: Clarendon Press (Oxford), 1961.
        Although this work contains no specific chapter
        on John Ruskin, its numerous references to
        John Ruskin make it a valuable source for ref-
        erence.

452   Fishman, Solomon. "John Ruskin." The Interpre-
      tation of Art: Essays on the Art Criticism of John
      Ruskin, Walter Pater, Clive Bell, Roger Fry and
      Herbert Read. Berkeley, Calif.: University of
      California Press, 1963, pp. 9-41.

453   Fitch, George Hamlin. "Ruskin the Apostle of
      Art." Modern English Books of Power. New York:
      Grosset and Dunlap, 1912, pp. 87-95.

454   Fitzhugh, Harriet Lloyd and Fitzhugh, P. K. Con-
      cise Biographical Dictionary of Famous Men and
      Women. Rev. and enl. ed. New York: Grosset
      and Dunlap, 1949, pp. 595-597.

455   Fleming, G. H. Rossetti and the Pre-Raphaelite
      Brotherhood. London: Rupert Hart-Davis, 1967.

456   Fredeman, William E. Pre-Raphaelitism: A Bib-
      liocritical Study. Cambridge, Mass.: Harvard
      University Press, 1965, pp. 183-185.

457   Frothingham, Paul Revere. "John Ruskin." All
      These. Cambridge, Mass.: Harvard University
      Press, 1927, pp. 73-102.

458   Gaunt, William. "Trials of a Prophet" and "But-
      terfly in the Box." Aesthetic Adventure. New

York: Harcourt, Brace, 1945, pp. 87-94 and 94-
113, respectively.

459 Gill, Eric. "John Ruskin." It All Goes Together:
Selected Essays. New York: Devin-Adair, 1944,
pp. 45-47.

460 Gladden, Washington. "Ruskin, the Preacher."
Witnesses of the Light. Boston: Houghton Mifflin,
1903, pp. 237-285. Facsimile ed.: Long Island:
Books for Libraries, 1969. (Essay Index Reprint
Series.)

461 Goodspeed, C. E. Yankee Bookseller. Boston:
Houghton Mifflin, 1938.

462 Green, Roger Lancelyn. Tellers of Tales. Enl.
ed. London: Ward, 1953, pp. 19-22.

463 Grether, Ewald Theophilus. "John Ruskin--John
A. Hobson." Essays in Social Economics in Honor
of Jessica Blanche Peixotto. Berkeley: University
of California Press, 1935, pp. 145-163.

464 Grigson, Geoffrey, and Gibbs-Smith, C. H., eds.
People. Windham, Conn.: Hawthorn, 1956, pp.
357-358.

465 Harrison, Frederic. "Ruskin as Master of Prose,"
"Ruskin as Prophet" and "Ruskin's Eightieth Birth-
day." Tennyson, Ruskin, Mill and Other Literary
Estimates. New York: Macmillan, 1900, pp. 48-
71, 72-97, and 98-103, respectively.

466 _____. "Fors Clavigera." Realities and Ideals:
Social Political, Literary and Artistic. London:
Macmillan, 1908, pp. 284-351.

467 _____. "Ruskin." Autobiographic Memoirs.
2 vols. London: Macmillan, 1911, vol. I, pp.
229-244.

468 _____. "Life of Ruskin." Among My Books:

Centenaries, Reviews, Memoirs. London: Macmillan, 1912, pp. 308-313.

469 Harrison, J. F. C. History of the Working Men's
     College. London: Routledge, 1954.

470 Hathaway, Esse Virginia. "Good Neighbors."
     Partners in Progress. New York: McGraw-Hill,
     1935, pp. 231-259.

471 Häusermann, Hans Walter. "Ruskin." The Gene-
     vese Background: Studies of Shelley, Francis Dan-
     by, Maria Edgeworth, Ruskin, Meredith, and
     Joseph Conrad in Geneva (with Hitherto Unpublished
     Letters). London: Routledge and Kegan Paul,
     1952, pp. 157-181.

472 Hillis, Newell Dwight. "John Ruskin." Great Men
     As Prophets of a New Era. New York: Revell,
     1922, pp. 190-216.

473 Hinchman, Walter Swain and Gummere, Francis
     Barton. "John Ruskin." Lives of Great English
     Writers from Chaucer to Browning. Boston:
     Houghton Mifflin, 1908, pp. 447-460.

474 Hitchcock, Henry Russell. "Ruskin and American
     Architecture: or Regeneration Long Delayed."
     Concerning Architecture: Essays on Architectural
     Writers and Writing Presented to Nikolaus Pevsner.
     Ed. John Newenham Summerson. Baltimore: Pen-
     guin Books, 1968, pp. 166-208.

475 Hough, G. "Ruskin." The Last Romantics. Lon-
     don: Gerald Duckworth, 1949. Reprinted: Lon-
     don: Methuen, 1961.

476 Hunt, William Holman. Pre-Raphaelitism and the
     Pre-Raphaelite Brotherhood. 2 vols. New York:
     Macmillan, 1905-1906.

477 Hutton, Richard Holt. "Why Mr. Ruskin Failed
     as a Poet." Brief Literary Criticisms. Ed.

E. M. Roscoe. London: Macmillan, 1906, pp.
347-354.

478 Inge, William Ralph. "Plato and Ruskin. " Essays
by Divers Hands, Being the Transactions of the
Society. vol. 14. Royal Society of Literature of
the United Kingdom, London. London: Oxford
University Press, 1933-1938, pp. 49-66.

479 Jackson, Holbrook. "John Ruskin. " Printing of
Books. New York: Scribner, 1939, pp. 81-87.

480 _____. "Ruskin. " Dreamers of Dreams: The
Rise and Fall of 19th Century Idealism. New York:
Farrar, Straus, 1949, pp. 93-133.

481 James, Henry. "Contemporary Notes on Whistler
and Ruskin. " Views and Reviews. Boston: Ball,
1908, pp. 207-214.

482 _____. "Ruskin's Collection of Drawings by
Turner" and "On Whistler and Ruskin. " Painter's
Eye: Notes and Essays on the Pictorial Arts.
Ed. John L. Sweeney. Cambridge, Mass. : Har-
vard University Press, 1956, pp. 158-160 and 172-
174, respectively.

483 Kazin, Alfred. "Writer and the Madman. " Inmost
Leaf: A Collection of Essays. New York: Harcourt, Brace, 1955, pp. 229-235.

484 Kimbrough, Robert. "Calm Between Crises: Pat-
tern and Direction in Ruskin's Mature Thought. "
British Victorian Literature: Recent Evaluations.
Ed. Shiv Kumar Kumar. New York: New York
University Press, 1969, pp. 345-356.

485 Klenze, Camillo von. "Romantic View of Art:
German Predecessors of Ruskin. " From Goethe
to Hauptmann: Studies in Changing Culture. New
York: Viking Press, 1926, pp. 67-102.

486 Lambert, R. Sir John Simon 1816-1904. London:

MacGibbon and Kee, 1963.

487 Lavrin, Janko. From Ruskin to Mayakovsky: A
     Study in the Evaluation of Literature. Philadelphia:
     Richard West, 1973 (reprint of 1948 edition).

488 Lee, Elizabeth. Mary Russell Mitford: Corres-
     pondence with Charles Boner and John Ruskin.
     London: Fisher Unwin, 1914. Chicago: Rand-
     McNally, 1915.

489 LeRoy, Gaylord C. "John Ruskin." Perplexed
     Prophets: Six Nineteenth-Century British Authors.
     Ed. Austin Wright. Philadelphia: University of
     Pennsylvania Press (for Temple University Publi-
     cations), 1953, pp. 86-103.

490 _____. "John Ruskin." Victorian Literature:
     Modern Essays in Criticism. Ed. Austin Wright.
     New York: Oxford University Press, 1961, pp.
     268-283.
         This essay was taken from Perplexed Prophets,
         entry no. 489.

491 Lindsay, Alexander Dunlop. "Social Conscience
     and the Ideas of Ruskin." Ideas and Beliefs of the
     Victorians: An Historical Revaluation of the Vic-
     torian Age. Chester Springs, Pa.: Dufour, 1959,
     pp. 277-282.

492 Links, J. G. Venice for Pleasure. London:
     Bodley Head, 1966.

493 Lippincott, Benjamin Evans. Victorian Critics of
     Democracy: Carlyle, Ruskin, Arnold, Stephen,
     Maine, Lecky. Minneapolis: The University of
     Minnesota Press, 1938, pp. 54-92. Reprinted:
     New York: Octagon Press, 1964.

494 Lodge, Oliver Joseph. "Ruskin's Political Econo-
     my." Modern Problems. London: Methuen,
     1912, pp. 272-284.

495   Lucas, Edward Verrall. "Fireworks--and a Law-
      suit." Saunterer's Rewards. Philadelphia: J. B.
      Lippincott, 1934, pp. 126-137.

496   Lutyens, Mary, ed. Effie in Venice. London:
      Murray, 1965.
          Reprinted in the U.S.A. as follows: Young
          Mrs. Ruskin in Venice: Unpublished Letters of
          Mrs. John Ruskin Written from Venice, Between
          1849-1852. New York: The Vanguard Press,
          1967.

497   Luxmoore, H. E. The Guild of St. George. Lon-
      don: George Allen and Unwin, 1925.

498   MacCarthy, Desmond. "Ruskin." Portraits. Lon-
      don: Macmillan, 1932, pp. 234-241. Reprinted:
      London: Oxford University Press, 1954.

499   McCarthy, Justin. "Ruskin and the Pre-Raphael-
      ites." Portraits of the Sixties. London: Unwin,
      1903, pp. 191-201.

500   MacDonald, Greville. George MacDonald and His
      Wife. London: George Allen and Unwin, 1924.

501   _____. Reminiscences of a Specialist. London:
      George Allen and Unwin, 1932.

502   Mackail, John William. "Ruskin." Studies in Hu-
      manism. London: Longmans, Green, 1938, pp.
      236-246.

503   McKenzie, Gordon. Critical Responsiveness: A
      Study of the Psychological Current in Later Eight-
      eenth-Century Criticism. Berkeley: University of
      California Press, 1949.

504   Magill, Frank Northern, ed. Cyclopedia of World
      Authors. New York: Harper, 1958, pp. 926-927.

505   Matthews, Brander. "Devil's Advocate." Gate-
      ways to Literature, and Other Essays. New York:

Scribner, 1912, pp. 93-112.

506   Meynell, Alice Christiana. "Seven Lamps of
      Architecture." Prose and Poetry: Centenary Vol-
      ume. Ed. Frederick Page. London: J. Cape,
      1947, pp. 333-343.

507   Miles, Josephine. The Pathetic Fallacy in the
      Nineteenth Century. Berkeley: University of Cal-
      ifornia Press, 1942. Reprinted: New York:
      Octagon Books, 1965.

508   Millett, Kate. "The Debate Over Women: Ruskin
      vs. Mill." Suffer and Be Still: Women in the Vic-
      torian Age. Ed. Martha Vicinus. Bloomington,
      Ind.: Indiana University Press, 1972, pp. 121-
      139.

509   Montgomery, Elizabeth Rider. The Story Behind
      Great Stories. New York: McBride, 1947, pp.
      61-65.

510   Mumby, F. A. and Stallybrass, F. H. S. From
      Swan Sonnenschein to George Allen and Unwin Ltd.
      London: George Allen and Unwin, 1955.

511   Murthi, A. N. S. Names You Should Know. Army
      Education Stores, 1954, pp. 102-109.

512   Nelson, Lawrence Emerson. "Wailers in the
      Wilderness." Our Roving Bible: Tracking Its In-
      fluence Through English and American Life. Nash-
      ville, Tenn.: Abingdon-Cokesbury, 1945, pp. 163-
      169.

513   Nevinson, Henry Woodd. "Last of the Prophets."
      Books and Personalities. New York: Lane, 1905,
      pp. 57-65

514   Norton, Sara. Letters of Charles Eliot Norton.
      2 vols. London: Constable, 1913.

515   Noyce, Wilfrid. Scholar Mountaineers. New York:

Roy Publishers, 1950, pp. 103-113.

516   Painter, G. D. "Salvation Through Ruskin."
      Proust: The Early Years. Boston: Little, Brown,
      1959.

517   Parrott, Thomas Marc and Martin, Robert Bernard.
      "John Ruskin." Companion to Victorian Literature.
      New York: Charles Scribner's Sons, 1955, pp.
      241-247.

518   Parry, Edward Abbott. "Concerning Whistler v.
      Ruskin." What the Judge Thought. London: Benn,
      1923, pp. 111-130.

519   Partington, W. Thomas J. Wise In the Original
      Cloth. London: Hale, 1946.

520   Pritchett, Victor Sawdon. "Victorian Child."
      Books in General. New York: Harcourt, 1953,
      pp. 56-61.

521   Proust, Marcel. Marcel Proust: A Selection from
      His Miscellaneous Writings. Trans. Gerard Hop-
      kins. London: 1950.

522   _____ . "Days of Reading." Essays on Lan-
      guage and Literature. Ed. J. L. Hevesi. Port
      Washington, N.Y.: Kennikat Press, 1967 (circa
      1947).
          Proust discusses "Of Kings' Treasuries."

523   Ritchie, Anne Isabella. Records of Tennyson,
      Ruskin and Browning. Port Washington, N.Y.:
      Kennikat Press, 1969 (reprint of 1899 edition; first
      published in 1892). New York: Benjamin Blom,
      (1974) (reprint of 1892 edition). Philadelphia:
      Richard West, (1974) (reprint of 1896 edition).
      Folcroft, Pa.: Folcroft Library Editions (1974)
      (reprint of 1899 edition).

524   Rives, Hallie Erminie and Forbush, G. E. John
      Book. New York: Beechhurst Press, 1947, pp.

221-222.

525   Robertson, John M.   "Ruskin."   Modern Humanists
      Reconsidered.   London: Watts, 1927.
         Refers to Modern Humanists.   London: Swan
      Sonnenschein, 1891.

526   Rosenberg, John D.   "Style and Sensibility in Rus-
      kin's Prose."   The Art of Victorian Prose.   Ed.
      George Levine and William Madden.   New York:
      1968, pp. 177-200.

527   Routh, Harold Victor.   "Culture Is Disconcerted by
      Civilization."   Towards the Twentieth Century:
      Essays in the Spiritual History of the Nineteenth.
      London: Macmillan, 1937, pp. 155-166.

528   Saintsbury, George Edward Bateman.   "Mr. Rus-
      kin."   Collected Essays and Papers, 1875-1923.
      4 vols.   New York: E. P. Dutton, 1923-1924, vol.
      2, pp. 300-311.

529   Schilling, Bernard Nicholas.   "Ruskin."   Human
      Dignity and the Great Victorians.   New York: Co-
      lumbia University Press, 1946, pp. 145-174.

530   Scott, William Thompson.   "Ruskin."   Chesterton,
      and Other Essays.   New York: Methodist Book
      Concern, 1912.

531   Shaw, George Bernard.   "Ruskin's Politics."
      Classics in Sociology: A Course of Selected Read-
      ing by Authorities.   New York: Philosophical Li-
      brary, 1960, pp. 173-181.

532   Shuster, George Nauman.   "Ruskin, Pater, and
      the Pre-Raphaelites."   The Catholic Spirit in Mod-
      ern English Literature.   London: Macmillan,
      1922, pp. 166-186.

533   Spender, John Alfred.   "Memorable Men."   Last
      Essays.   Toronto: Cassell, 1944, pp. 32-39.

534 Spielmann, M. H. and Layard, G. S. Kate Greenaway. London: Black, 1905.

535 Squire, John Collings. "Ruskin: Feb., 1919."
Books in General. 1st-3rd series, 3 vols. London: Heinemann, 1919-1921, 3rd series, pp. 105-
109.

536 Stephen, Leslie. "John Ruskin." Studies of a
Biographer. 2nd series, vol. III. London: Duckworth, 1902, pp. 78-110.

537 Stewart, I. R. G. The Love That Was Stronger:
Lilias Trotter of Algiers. London: Lutterworth,
no date.

538 Sussman, Herbert L. "Art and the Machine:
John Ruskin." Victorians and the Machine: The
Literary Response to Technology. Cambridge,
Mass.: Harvard University Press, 1951 (reprinted
in 1968).

539 Tawney, R. H. "John Ruskin." Radical Tradition:
Twelve Essays on Politics, Education, and Literature. Ed. Rita Hinden. London: Penguin Books,
1966, pp. 42-46.

540 Thompson, Francis. "Academy Portrait XXXVIII."
Literary Criticisms: Newly Discovered and Col-
lected. Ed. Terence L. Connolly. New York:
E. P. Dutton, 1948, pp. 218-223.

541 Thompson, Laurence Victor, ed. Blue Plaque
Guide to Historic London Houses and the Lives of
Their Famous Residents. London: Newman
Neame, 1953.

542 Todd, W. B., ed. Thomas J. Wise Centenary
Studies. Austin, Texas: University of Texas
Press, 1959.

543 Tomlinson, Henry Major. "Ruskin." Waiting for
Daylight. New York: Knopf, 1922, pp. 140-146.

544   Unwin, Stanley. The Truth About a Publisher.
      London: George Allen and Unwin, 1960.

545   Vanderbilt, K. Charles Eliot Norton. Cambridge,
      Mass. : Belknap Press, 1959.

546   Van Doren, Charles, ed. Letters to Mother.
      Great Neck, N. Y. : Channel, 1959, pp. 31-34.

547   Van Dyke, John Charles. "John Ruskin. " Warner
      Library. 30 vols. Ed. John William Cunliffe and
      Ashley Horace Thorndike. U. S. Publishers Asso-
      ciation, 1917, vol. 12.

548   _____ "John Ruskin. " Columbia University
      Course in Literature, Based on the World's Best
      Literature. 18 vols. Ed. John William Cunliffe.
      New York: Columbia University Press, 1928-1929,
      vol. 13.

549   Wagner, Anthony Richard. "Coat of Arms of John
      Ruskin. " Historic Heraldry of Britain: An Illus-
      trated Series of British Historical Arms, With
      Notes, Glossary and an Introduction to Heraldry.
      London: Oxford University Press, 1939.

550   Walker, Janie. "John Ruskin. " Stories of the
      Victorian Writers. London: Macmillan, 1922, pp.
      23-33.

551   Wallace, Archer. "Religious Faith of Great Phi-
      losophers. " Religious Faith of Great Men. New
      York: Round Table Press, 1934, pp. 94-113.

552   Wallas, Graham. "John Ruskin. " Men and Ideas:
      Essays. New York: Norton, 1940, pp. 75-80.

553   Ward, M. A. "John Ruskin as Social Reformer. "
      Prophets of the Nineteenth Century: Carlyle, Rus-
      kin, Tolstoi. London: Gay and Bird, 1900, pp.
      83-133.

554   Webling, P. Peggy: The Story of One Score Year

and Ten. London: Hutchinson, no date.

555 Whitehouse, John Howard. "John Ruskin." Great
Democrats. Ed. Alfred Barratt Brown. London:
Nicholson, 1934, pp. 569-584.

556 Wilenski, Reginald Howard. "Technique of the
Pre-Raphaelites: The Daguerrotype and Ruskin."
The Modern Movement in Art. London: Faber,
1927 (rev. ed. published in 1935).

557   . "John Ruskin." The Great Victorians.
Ed. Harold John Massingham and Hugh Massingham.
London: Nicholson and Watson, 1932, pp. 407-421.

558 Williams, Raymond. "Art and Society." Culture
and Society, 1780-1950. New York: Columbia
University Press, 1958, pp. 130-158.

559 Winchester, Caleb Thomas. "John Ruskin." Old
Castle, and Other Essays. London: Macmillan,
1922, pp. 267-290.

560 Woodberry, George Edward. "Mr. Ruskin's Early
Years." Literary Memoirs of the Nineteenth Century. New York: Harcourt, Brace, 1921, pp.
135-144.

561 Woolf, Virginia Stephen. "Ruskin." The Captain's
Deathbed. New York: Harcourt, Brace, 1950, pp.
48-52.

562   . "Ruskin." Collected Essays. 4 vols.
New York: Harcourt, Brace and World, 1966,
vol. I, pp. 205-208.

563 Wordsworth, Elizabeth. "John Ruskin." Essays
Old and New. London: Oxford University Press,
1919, pp. 80-94.

564 Young, George Malcolm. "Eyes and No Eyes."
Last Essays. London: Rupert Hart-Davis, 1950,
pp. 130-135.

565   Young, M. F.   The Letters of a Noble Woman
       (Mrs. La Touche of Harristown).   London: Allen,
       1908.

PART II

PERIODICALS

A. CORRESPONDENCE AND ONE EDITED ESSAY

566   Bradley, John Lewis. "An Unpublished Ruskin Letter to Mrs. John Simon." _Burlington Magazine_, 100 (Jan. 1958), 25-26.

567   . "Ruskin's Advice to an Amateur Artist: Some New Letters to Louisa, Marchioness of Waterford." _Studies in English Literature, 1500-1900_, 1 (Autumn 1961), 101-122.

568   Coulling, Sidney M. B. "Two Unpublished Letters of John Ruskin to Edward Clayton." _Huntington Library Quarterly_, 27 (1963-1964), 87-92.

569   DeLaura, David J. "Ruskin and the Brownings: Twenty-Five Unpublished Letters." _Bulletin of the John Rylands Library_, 54 (Spring 1972), 314-356.

570   Dougherty, Charles T. "Ruskin and Manning: Some New Ruskin Letters." _Manuscripta_, 10 (1966), 164-168.

571   Ferguson, Oliver W. "Ruskin's Continental Letters to Mrs. Severn, 1888." _Journal of English and Germanic Philology_, 51 (Oct. 1952), 527-536.

572   Fogle, French. "Unpublished Letters of Ruskin and Millais 1854-1855." _Huntington Library Quarterly_, 20 (1956-1957), 39-54.

573   Fotheringham, J. T. "Some Ruskin Letters Hitherto Unpublished." _Vassar Journal of Undergraduate Studies_, 1 (May 1926), 231.

574   James, William Milburne.   "Ruskin and Effie Gray:
       Extracts from an Unpublished Correspondence."
       Cornhill Magazine, 162 (Winter 1946), 163-178 and
       (Spring 1947), 258-274.

575   Kaufman, Paul.   "John Ruskin to Rawdon Brown:
       The Unpublished Correspondence of an Anglo-Vene-
       tian Friendship."   North American Review, (Sept. -
       Nov. 1925 and Dec. -Jan. 1925-1926).

576   "Lamp of Memory."   Ed. Charles Wright Thomas.
       Chautauquan, 62:404.   (essay)
              Also in Essays in Contemporary Civilization.
              Ed. Charles Wright Thomas.   See "Lamp of
              Memory," entry no. 170.

577   Landow, George P.   "John Ruskin and W. J. Lin-
       ton: A New Letter."   English Language Notes, 10
       (Sept. 1972), 38-41.

578   .   "'I heard of a delightful ghost': A New
       Ruskin Letter."   Philological Quarterly, 52 (Oct.
       1973), 779-783.

579   . Mahl, Mary R. , and Maidmont, B. E.
       "Ruskin Letters."   Notes and Queries, 216 (Nov.
       1972), 419-421.

580   "Letters of John Ruskin."   Bulletin of the John
       Rylands Library, 36 (Sept. 1953), 3-9.

581   "Letters of Ruskin and Carlyle."   Bulletin of the
       John Rylands Library, 40 (1957), 3-4.

582   Liversidge, M. J. H.   "John Ruskin and William
       Boxall: An Unpublished Correspondence."   Apollo,
       85 (Jan. 1967), 39-44.

583   "Mr. Ruskin's Illness as Described by Himself."
       British Medical Journal, 1 (1900), 225-226.

584   Quennell, Peter.   "Ruskin and the Women."   At-
       lantic Monthly, 179 (Feb. 1947), 37-45. (unpublished
       letters)

585   "Ruskin in Old Age: Some Unpublished Letters. "
      Ed. John Howard Whitehouse.   Scribner's Magazine,
      62 (Dec. 1917), 738-748.

586   "Ruskin Letters and Papers. " Bulletin of the John
      Rylands Library, 42 (1959), 1-4, 271-273.

587   Skelton, Robin. "John Ruskin: The Final Years:
      A Survey of the Ruskin Correspondence in the John
      Rylands Library. " Bulletin of the John Rylands Li-
      brary, 37 (March 1955), 562-586.

588   Spence, Margaret E.   "Ruskin's Correspondence
      with Miss Blanche Atkinson. " Bulletin of the John
      Rylands Library, 42 (Sept. 1959), 194-219.

589   _____. "Ruskin's Correspondence with His God-
      Daughter, Constance Oldham. " Bulletin of the John
      Rylands Library, 43 (March 1961), 520-537.

590   Williams, R. E. T.   "Three Ruskin Letters. "
      Notes and Queries, 10 (Jan. 1963), 23-24.

B. CRITICISM AND SCHOLARSHIP

1. Biographical

591 Anonymous. "If Sex Were All." Time, 92 (Dec. 27, 1968), 62-63.

592 Bragman, Louis J. "The Case of John Ruskin: A Study in Cyclothymia." The American Journal of Psychiatry, 91 (March 1935), 1137-1159.

593 Burd, Van Akin. "Ruskin's Defense of Turner: The Imitative Phase." Philological Quarterly, 37 (Oct. 1958), 465-483.
The reality of John Ruskin's thought as a youth is discussed in contrast with Ruskin's recollections in Praeterita.

594 Carmichael, Alexander G. "The Ruskins." Celtic Review, 2 (April 16, 1906), 343-351.

595 Clements, Richard. "John Ruskin: Social Reformer." Social Service Quarterly, 45 (Oct. /Dec. 1971), 46-49.

596 Collingwood, William Gersham. "Ruskin's Music" (Oct. 1902), "Ruskin's Maps" (Dec. 1902), "Ruskin's Bibles" (Jan. 1903), "Ruskin's Library" (Feb. 1903), "Ruskin's Old Road" (May 1903), "Ruskin's Cash-book" (June 1903), "Ruskin's Jewels" (Aug. 1903), "Ruskin's Hand" (Sept. 1903), "Ruskin's Gardening" (Oct. 1903). Good Words.
The other articles of this series are listed in entry no. 727.

597   Cook, Edward Tyas.   "Ruskin and His Books: An
      Interview with His Publisher."   Strand Magazine,
      24 (Dec. 1902), 709.

598   Davis, Kenneth W.   "A Note on the Ruskin-Black-
      wood's Controversy."   Victorian Newsletter, 30
      (1966), 26-27.

599   Dearden, James S.   "Some Portraits of John Rus-
      kin in the Ruskin Galleries, Bembridge School,
      Isle of Wight and Brantwood, Coniston."   Apollo,
      72 (Dec. 1960), 190-195.

600   _____.   "Further Portraits of John Ruskin."
      Apollo, 74 (June 1961), 171-178.

601   _____.   "Ruskin on Tour in Northern England
      and Scotland in 1838."   Apollo, 78 (Aug. 1963),
      129-132.

602   _____.   "John Ruskin's Bookplates."   Book Col-
      lector, 13 (Autumn 1964), 335-339.

603   _____.   "John Ruskin, the Collector: With a
      Catalogue of the Illuminated and Other Manuscripts
      Formerly in His Collection."   Library, 21 (1966),
      124-154.

604   _____.   "John Ruskin's Tour to the Lake Dis-
      trict in 1837."   Connoisseur, 167 (March 1968),
      165-168.

605   _____.   "Edward Burne-Jones--Designer to John
      Ruskin."   Connoisseur, 170 (Feb. 1969), 89-94.

606   _____.   "John Ruskin's Art Collection--a Cen-
      tenary."   Burlington Magazine, 113 (Aug. 1971),
      27-31.

607   _____.   "Portrait of a Bibliophile: John Rus-
      kin, 1819-1900."   Book Collector, 21 (Summer
      1972), 203-213.

608   Emslie, J. P. "Recollections of Ruskin." Work-
       ing Men's College Journal, 10 (1908), 322 and 341.

609   Fain, John Tyree. "Ruskin and His Father."
       PMLA, 54 (1944), 236-243.

610   Fenn, W. W. "Ruskin and Millais in Scotland:
       A Memory of Ruskin." Chambers's Journal, 8
       (Sept. 1905), 645-647.

611   Gale, C. F. "At Canterbury and Amiens with
       John Ruskin." Cornhill Magazine, 119 (Feb.
       1913).

612   H. "Mr. Ruskin's Illness." British Medical Jour-
       nal, (Jan. 27, 1900), 225.
          Joan Evans in a footnote on page 426 in the
          bibliography of her book John Ruskin (see entry
          no. 314) writes that "H." is "probably George
          Harley, F. R. S."

613   Holroyd, Michael. "John Ruskin's Brantwood
       Diary." Spectator, 227 (July 24, 1971), 137-138.

614   Incrapers, Nicolò. "Ruskin in Venice." Annali
       della facolta di magistero, 3 (1961-1962), 121-125.

615   Joseph, Robert J. "John Ruskin: Radical and
       Psychotic Genius." Psychoanalytic Review, 56
       (1969), 425-441.

616   Lewis, Naomi. "A Camberwell Beauty." En-
       counter, 25 (Aug. 1965), 76-79.
          The "Beauty" is Effie Ruskin.

617   Lutyens, Mary. "The Millais-La Touche Corres-
       pondence." Cornhill, 1051 (Spring 1967), 1-18.

618   _____. "Millais's Portrait of Ruskin." Apollo,
       85 (April 1967), 246-253.

619   _____. "Where Did Ruskin Sleep?" The Times
       Literary Supplement, 68 (Jan. 2, 1969), 17.

Lutyens provides insight into the Ruskin-Gray-
Millais triangle with this discussion of the un-
usual sleeping arrangements John Ruskin devised
when they went on holiday together in 1853.

620 Maidmont, B. E. "'Only Print': Ruskin and the
Publishers." Durham University Journal, 63 (June
1971), 196-207.

621 _____. "Author and Publisher: John Ruskin
and George Allen, 1890-1900." Business Archives,
36 (June 1972), 21-32.

622 Mumm, A. L. "Ruskin and the Alps." Alpine
Journal, 32 (1919), 328.

623 Notice of Ruskin's Death and Career. Literary
Year Book, (1901).

624 Plumb, J. H. "Grounds for Divorce." Horizon,
11 (Autumn 1969), 29.

625 "Portrait by J. E. Millais." Illustrated London
News, 227 (Oct. 15, 1955), 671.

626 Pritchett, V. S. "Ruskin and the Girls." New
Statesman, 79 (Feb. 27, 1970), 294-295.

627 Quennell, Peter. "Education of an Aesthete."
Cornhill Magazine, 162 (Spring 1947), 240-257 and
(Summer 1947), 365-375.

628 _____. "Ruskin: The Middle Years." Cornhill Magazine, 163 (Spring 1948), 93-108.

629 _____. "Ruskin--Love and Economics." Cornhill Magazine, 163 (Summer 1948), 314-331.

630 _____. "Ruskin and Rose La Touche." Cornhill Magazine, 163 (Fall 1948), 404-410.

631 "Ruskin in Verona." Burlington Magazine, 108
(July 1966), 393.

632 "Ruskin in Verona. " Apollo, 84 (Sept. 1966), 233.

633 "Ruskin Lecturing at Oxford: Pencil Sketch by
D. S. MacColl. " Studio, 132 (Dec. 1946), 179.

634 "The Ruskin Statue. " International Studio, 61
(March 1917), xxxiv.

635 Russell, J. Almus. "Ruskin the Professor. "
South Atlantic Quarterly, 27 (1928), 88-95.

636 _____. "Ruskin's Process of Education. " Pro-
gressive Teacher, (Sept. 1928), 10-42 and (Oct.
1928), 16-38.

637 _____. "Ruskin the Educator. " Education, 49
(Dec. 1928), 245-252.

638 Scott, Walter S. "Ruskin and Rosie La Touche. "
Quarterly Review, 286 (April 1948), 204-218.

639 _____. "Ruskin's Parents. " Quarterly Review,
286 (Oct. 1948), 455-468.

640 Shipp, Horace. "Ruskin Versus Whistler. " Apollo,
72 (Sept. 1960), 61-62.

641 Spence, Margaret E. "Ruskin's Friendship with
Mrs. Fanny Talbot. " Bulletin of the John Rylands
Library, 42 (March 1960).

642 Sutcliffe, F. M. "Photographer to John Ruskin. "
Photographic Journal, (June 1931), 255.

643 Swanson, Donald R. "Ruskin and His 'Master. '"
Victorian Newsletter, 31 (1967), 56-59.

644 Wallis, Nevile. "Turner and Ruskin: A Study of
Their Relationship. " Times Educational Supplement, 41 (May 18, 1951), 390.

645 Whittingham, Selby. "Turner, Ruskin and Constable at Salisbury. " Burlington Magazine, 113 (May

1971), 272-275.

646 Zorzi, A. "Ruskin in Venice." Cornhill Magazine, 121 (Aug. and Sept. 1906), 250-265 and 366-380.

2. Background of Ruskin and Influences on Him

647 Allentuck, Marcia Epstein. "William Holman Hunt, Monk and Ruskin: An Unpublished Letter." Apollo, 97 (Feb. 1973), 156-157.

648 Angus, Douglas R. "The Relationship of Wordsworth's Ode on the Intimations of Immortality to Ruskin's Theory of the Infinite in Art." Modern Language Review, 36 (Oct. 1941), 506-508.

649 _____. "Wordsworth and Other Influences on the Development of Impressionism in Ruskin's Modern Painters." Ohio State University Abstracts of Doctors' Dissertations, 35 (1941), 3-7.

650 Anonymous. "Greek Evangelistarium from the Library of John Ruskin." British Museum Quarterly, 5 (Dec. 1930), 87.

651 Burd, Van Akin. "Background to Modern Painters: The Tradition and the Turner Controversy." PMLA, 74 (June 1959), 254-267.

652 Cate, G. Allen. "The Correspondence of Thomas Carlyle and John Ruskin." Dissertation Abstracts, 28 (1967), 4120A (Duke).

653 Christian, J. "Early German Sources for Pre-Raphaelite Designs." Art Quarterly, 36 (Spring-Summer 1973), 276-286.

654 Fitch, Raymond Edward. "The Golden Furrow:

John Ruskin and the Greek Religion. " Dissertation Abstracts, 26 (1965), 7315 (Penn.).

655   Fulford, R.   "Ruskin's Notes on Carlyle. " Times Literary Supplement, 70 (April 16, 1971), 453.

656   Gilbert, Katharine.   "Ruskin's Relation to Aristotle. " Philosophical Review, 49 (1940), 52-62.

657   Goldberg, M. H.   "Carlyle and Ruskin. " Times Literary Supplement, 34 (May 1935), 313.

658   Herrmann, Luke.   "Ruskin and Turner: A Riddle Resolved. " Burlington Magazine, 112 (Oct. 1970), 696-699.

659   Hough, G.   "Ruskin and Roger Fry. " Cambridge Journal, 1 (1947), 14.

660   Inge, W. R.   "Plato and Ruskin. " Transactions, Royal Society of Literature, 14 (1935).

661   Kaufman, Paul.   "Rawdon Brown and His Adventures in Venetian Archives. " English Miscellany (Rome), 18 (1967), 283-302.

662   Kegel, Charles H.   "Carlyle and Ruskin: An Influential Friendship. " Brigham Young University Studies, 5 (1964), 219-229.

663   Logan, James V.   "Wordsworth and the Pathetic Fallacy. " Modern Language Notes, 55 (1940), 187-191.

664   O'Connor, Peter.   "An Unpublished Letter from J. A. Froude to Ruskin. " Notes and Queries, 11 (June 1964), 233-234.

665   Penny, Nicholas.   "John Ruskin and Tintoretto. " Apollo, 99 (April 1974), 268-273.

666   Robertson, Alex.   "Ruskin and Venice. " Good Words, (July 1900).

667   Sanders, Charles Richard. "Carlyle's Letters to
       Ruskin: A Finding List with Some Unpublished
       Letters and Comments. " Bulletin of the John Ry-
       lands Library, 41 (Sept. 1958), 208-238.

668   Scott, W. S. "John Ruskin's Parents. " Quarterly
       Review, 286 (Oct. 1948), 455-468.

669   Shapiro, Harold I. "The Poetry of Architecture:
       Ruskin's Preparation for Modern Painters. " Ren-
       aissance and Modern Studies, 15 (1971), 70-84.

670   Sinclair, William. "The Scottish Ancestors of
       Ruskin. " St. George, 9 (Oct. 1906), 238-247.

671   Sturge Moore, T. and Sturge Moore, D. "John
       Ruskin's Parents. " Quarterly Review, 287 (1948),
       455.

672   Unrau, John. "A Note on Ruskin's Reading of
       Pugin. " English Studies, 48 (1967), 339-347.

673   _____. "Ethics and Architecture: Some Pre-
       cursors of Pugin and Ruskin. " Notes and Queries,
       21 (May 1974), 174-175.

3. Ruskin's Reputation and Influence

a. Contemporaries

674   Antippas, A. P. "Browning's 'The Guardian An-
       gel': A Possible Early Reference to Ruskin. "
       Victorian Poetry, 11 (Winter 1973), 342-344.

675   Birkenhead, Sheila. "Ruskin and Harristown. "
       County Kildare Archaeological Society Journal, 14
       (1966-1967), 152-162.

676   Braam, J. W. "The Ruskin Co-operative Colony."
      American Journal of Sociology, 8 (1903), 667-680.

677   C., O. "Ruskin, Acland and the Oxford Museum."
      Harlequin, (June 22, 1950), 18.

678   Clark, W. "Ruskin and Modern Business." Spec-
      tator, 84 (Feb. 1900).

679   Cook, Edward Tyas. "Ruskin and the New Liberal-
      ism." New Liberal Review, 1 (Feb. 1901), 18-25.

680   Davis, W. G. "The Failure of the Ruskin Colony."
      Gunton's Magazine, 21 (1901).

681   Dearden, James S. "The Ruskin Circle in Italy in
      1872." Connoisseur, 179 (April 1972), 240-245.

682   Dolk, Lester. "The Reception of Modern Painters."
      Modern Language Notes, 57 (1942), 621-626.

683   Fain, John Tyree. "Ruskin and the Orthodox Po-
      litical Economists." Southern Economic Journal,
      10 (1943), 1-13.

684   _____. "Ruskin and Mill." Modern Language
      Quarterly, 12 (June 1951), 150-154.

685   _____. "Ruskin and Hobson." PMLA, 67
      (1952), 297-307.

686   Feltes, N. "George Eliot's 'Pier Glass': The
      Development of a Metaphor." Modern Philology,
      67 (1969-1970), 69-71.

687   Fike, Francis George, Jr. "The Influence of John
      Ruskin upon the Aesthetic Theory and Practice of
      Gerard Manley Hopkins." Dissertation Abstracts,
      25 (1964), 1208 (Stanford).

688   Gerdts, William H. "Influence of Ruskin and Pre-
      Raphaelitism on American Still-Life Painting."
      American Art Journal, 1 (Fall 1969), 80-97.

689   Greenberg, Robert A.   "Ruskin, Pugin, and the
      Contemporary Context of 'The Bishop Orders His
      Tomb.'"   PMLA, 84 (1969), 1588-1594.
          Greenberg discusses Browning and what he owed
      to the influence of John Ruskin and Pugin.

690   Herford, C. H.   "Ruskin and the Gothic Revival."
      Quarterly Review, 206 (1907), 77-96.

691   Ironside, Robin.   "Pre-Raphaelite Paintings at
      Wallington: A Note on William Bell Scott and Rus-
      king."   Architectural Review, 92 (Dec. 1942), 147-
      149.

692   Jump, J. D.   "Ruskin's Reputation in the Eighteen-
      Fifties: The Evidence of the Three Principal Week-
      lies."   PMLA, 63 (June 1948), 679-685.

693   Kegel, Charles H.   "Ruskin's St. George in Amer-
      ica."   American Quarterly, 9 (1957), 412-440.
          This article is about Julius Augustus Wayland,
      who established the Ruskin Co-operative Associa-
      tion near Tennessee City, Tennessee, and about
      the Association itself.

694   Kinch, Richard W.   "The Aesthetic of Truth to
      Nature: A Study in Victorian Realism, 1846-1860."
      Dissertation Abstracts, 29 (1968), 4459A (Kent
      State).
          Kinch writes that Ruskin's Modern Painters and
      other critics "provide a rationale for Victorian
      pictorial realism."

695   Kitson, Michael.   "Ruskin and English Taste."
      Listener, 87 (Feb. 17, 1972), 205-207.

696   Kotzin, Michael.   "Pre-Raphaelitism, Ruskinism,
      and French Symbolism."   Art Journal, 25 (Sum-
      mer 1966), 347-350.

697   LeRoy, Gaylord C.   "John Ruskin: An Interpreta-
      tion of His 'Daily Maddening Rage.'"   Modern Lan-
      guage Quarterly, 10 (March 1949), 81-88.

698   Martineau, G. D.   "Guild of St. George."   Spec-
      tator, 182 (June 10, 1949), 781.

699   Maslenikov, Oleg A.   "Ruskin, Bely, and the
      Solovyovs."   Slavonic and East European Review,
      34 (Dec. 1956), 15-23.

700   Parkes, Kineton.   "Ruskin and Pre-Raphaelitism."
      New Century Review, 7 (Feb. 1900), 133-143.

701   Reynolds, Graham.   "Pre-Raphaelites and Their
      Circle."   Apollo, 93 (June 1971), 494-501.

702   Roberts, K.   "Ruskin and His Circle at St. James's
      Square."   Burlington Magazine, 106 (Feb. 1964),
      91.

703   Smallwood, Osborn T.   "John Ruskin and the Ox-
      ford Movement."   College Language Association
      Journal, 3 (Dec. 1959), 114-118.

704   Spence, Margaret E.   "The Guild of St. George:
      Ruskin's Attempt to Translate His Ideas into Prac-
      tice."   Bulletin of the John Rylands Library, 40
      (Sept. 1957), 147-201.

705   Steegman, John.   "Lord Lindsay's History of
      Christian Art."   Warburg and Courtland Institute
      Journal, 10 (1947), 123-131.
         Steegman discusses John Ruskin's review of
      Lord Lindsay's work and the ensuing controversy.

706   Surtees, Virginia.   "Godfather to Venice."   Times
      Literary Supplement, 64 (Jan. 28, 1965), 76.

707   Templeman, William D.   "Ruskin's Ploughshare
      and Hopkins' 'The Windhover.'"   English Studies,
      43 (1962), 103-106.

708   Wright, W. C.   "Hazlitt, Ruskin, and Nineteenth-
      Century Art Criticism."   Journal of Aesthetics and
      Art Criticism, 32 (Summer 1974), 509-523.

3b. 20th Century

709   Bentley, John A. "Ruskin and Modern Fiction."
      Queen's Quarterly, 29 (Feb. 1932), 145-156.

710   Dearden, James S. "The Production and Distribu-
      tion of John Ruskin's Poems 1850." Book Col-
      lector, 17 (Summer 1968), 151-167.
         Dearden catalogues extant copies and verifies
      the publication of only fifty copies of Poems.
      He examines how T. J. Wise knew this.

711   _____. "Wise and Ruskin." Book Collector,
      18 (Spring 1969), 45-56; (Summer 1969), 170-188;
      (Autumn 1969), 318-339.

712   _____. "The Haddon C. Adams Ruskin Collec-
      tion at Bembridge." John Rylands Library Bulle-
      tin, 55 (Spring 1973), 300-323.

713   Dougherty, Charles T. "Joyce and Ruskin."
      Notes and Queries, 198 (Feb. 1953), 76-77.

714   French, H. D. "The Charles Eliot Goodspeed Col-
      lection of Ruskin and Ruskiniana." Friends of
      Wellesley College Library Bulletin, 9 (1951).

715   Hendrick, G. "The Influence of Ruskin's Unto this
      Last on Gandhi." Ball State Teachers College
      Forum, 1 (Spring 1960), 67-72.

716   Hogan, Charles B. "The Yale Collection of the
      Manuscripts of John Ruskin." Yale University Li-
      brary Gazette, 16 (1942), 61-69.

717   Kay-Scott, Cyril. "Ruskin's Blight." Art Digest,
      6 (Sept. 1932), 26.

718   Lees-Milne, J. "Ruskin on Architecture: His
      Thought and Influence." Apollo, 99 (May 1974),
      385.

719   "Mr. Ruskin's Tea Shop: Marylebone Survival of
       a Brave Experiment." Times, (Feb. 26, 1957),
       10.

720   Murray, J. D.   "Marcel Proust as Critic and
       Disciple of Ruskin." Nineteenth Century, 101
       (April 1927), 614-619.

721   Russell, J. A.   "Ruskin's Influence on Present
       Day Thought." Education, 48 (Sept. 1927), 1-11.

722   Salomon, Louis B.   "The Pound-Ruskin Axis."
       College English, 16 (1954-1955), 270-276.

723   Talbey, Paul M.   "Architecture as Edward Gordon
       Craig's Interim Symbol: Ruskin and Other Influ-
       ences." Education Theatre Journal, 19 (March
       1967), 52-60.

4.   Ruskin's Work

a.   Written

724   Brown, S. E.   "The Unpublished Passages in the
       Manuscript of Ruskin's Autobiography." Victorian
       Newsletter, 16 (Fall 1959), 10-18.

725   Burd, Van Akin.   "Another Light on the Writing
       of Modern Painters." PMLA, 68 (1953), 755-763.

726   Clay, M. E.   "Ruskin and the N. R. A. : Analysis
       of the Essay on Work." Education, 54 (Jan. 1934),
       261-264.

727   Collingwood, William Gersham.   "Ruskin's 'Isola'"
       (Feb. 1902) and "Ruskin's 'Glaria'" (April 1902).
       Good Words.
           The other articles of this series are listed in
           entry no. 596.

728   Cranston, Maurice. "Ruskin's Letters to English
      Working Men. " Listener, 57 (Jan. 31, 1957), 192-
      193.

729   Durrant, William Scott. "From Art to Social Re-
      form: Ruskin's 'Nature of Gothic. '" Nineteenth
      Century, 67 (May 1910), 922-930.

730   Feltes, N. N. "The Quickest Hedge: Ruskin's
      Early Prose. " Victorian Newsletter, 34 (1968),
      18-22.

731   Flood, Ralph J. "Style as Meaning in Ruskin's
      Fors Clavigera. " Dissertation Abstracts, 29 (1968),
      2258A-2259A (Pennsylvania).

732   Hough, Graham. "Kata Phusin: Centenary of The
      Seven Lamps of Architecture. " Architectural Re-
      view, 106 (Nov. 1949), 279-282.

733   Ironside, R. "The Art of Criticism of John Rus-
      kin. " Horizon, 8 (July 1943), 8.

734   Landow, George P. "The Aesthetic Theories in
      John Ruskin's Modern Painters. " Dissertation Ab-
      stracts, 27 (1966), 3873A-3874A (Princeton).

735   _____. "Ruskin's Refutation of 'False Opinions
      Held Concerning Beauty. '" British Journal of Aes-
      thetics, 8 (Jan. 1968), 60-72.

736   _____. "Ruskin's Revision of the Third Edition
      of Modern Painters, Volume 1. " Victorian News-
      letter, 33 (Spring 1968), 12-16.

737   Levin, Gerold. "The Imagery of Ruskin's 'A Walk
      in Chamouni. '" Victorian Poetry, 5 (1967), 283-
      290.

738   Reynolds, E. E. "Unto this Last. " John O'Lon-
      don's, 3 (Oct. 1960), 411.

739   Rosenberg, John D. "The Geopoetry of John Rus-
      kin. " Etudes Anglaises, 22 (1969), 42-48.

740   Thorp, Willard.   "The Ruskin Manuscripts."
      Princeton University Library Chronicle, 1 (Feb.
      1940), 1-10.
         This is a bibliographic article.

4b.   Visual Art

741   Cook, Edward Tyas.   "Ruskin as Artist and Art
      Critic."   International Studio, 10 (April 1900), 77-
      92.

742   Davis, Frank.   "Looking Back at Drawings by
      John Ruskin."   Illustrated London News, (Sept. 3,
      1960), 394-395.

743   Dearden, James S.   "The Cunliffe Collection of
      Ruskin Drawings."   The Connoisseur, 171 (Aug.
      1969), 237-240.

744   Evans, Joan.   "John Ruskin as Artist."   Apollo,
      66 (Dec. 1957), 139-145.

745   Gibbons, F.   "Alpine Lake."   Princeton University
      Art Museum Record, 27 (1968), 86-87.

746   "Matterhorn: Siena."   Harvard University Fogg
      Art Museum Notes, 2 (Nov. 1927), 115.

747   Rocke, N.   "Ruskin Drawings for Italy."   Connois-
      seur, 90 (Aug. 1932), 132.

748   "Roving Kind: Exhibition of Drawings at Leighton
      House, Kensington."   Art News, 54 (April 1955),
      59.

749   Walton, P. H.   "Seven Ruskin Drawings in the
      Fogg Art Museum."   Harvard Library Bulletin, 14
      (1960), 265.

750   Walton, Paul. "A Water-Colour by John Ruskin:
      Amalfi." Burlington Magazine, 104 (Jan. 1962).

751   Whitehouse, John Howard. "Ruskin's First Sketch-
      Book." The Beacon, 2 (1923), 275.

5. Ruskin's Viewpoints and Philosophies

752   Alexander, Edward. "Ruskin and Science." Mod-
      ern Language Review, 64 (July 1969), 508-521.

753   Alford, John. "Romanticism via Ruskin." Art
      News, 42 (Dec. 1, 1943), 10-13.

754   Ames, Alfred C. "The Gospel in a Line by Rus-
      kin." American Friend, 33 (1945), 71.

755   Armytage, W. H. G. "Ruskin as Utopist." Notes
      and Queries, 3 (May 1956), 219-224.

756   Beard, Charles A. "Ruskin and the Babble of
      Tongues." The New Republic, 87 (Aug. 5, 1936),
      370-372.

757   Bond, Warwick. "Ruskin's Views of Literature."
      Contemporary Review, 77 (1905), 844.

758   Burd, Van Akin. "Ruskin's Quest for a Theory of
      Imagination." Modern Language Quarterly, 17
      (1956), 60-72.

759   _____. "Ruskin's Antidote for Carlyle's Purges."
      Boston University Studies in English, 3 (1957), 51-
      57.
      Burd examines John Ruskin's attitudes toward
      his girl pupils and toward Carlyle through vari-
      ant transcriptions of a letter from Carlyle to
      Ruskin.

760   Chianese, Robert L.   "The Development of Mod-
      ern Painters: The Growth of the Critic's Mind."
      Dissertation Abstracts, 32 (1971), 5175A-5176A
      (Washington).

761   Collet, C. E.   "The Development of Ruskin's
      Views on Interest." Economic Journal, (Jan. 1926)
      23-33.

762   Devereux, A. F. X.   "John Ruskin Economist."
      Catholic World, 108 (Feb. 1919), 628-641.

763   Dollarhide, Louis E.   "The Paradox of Ruskin's
      Admiration of Renaissance English Writers." Uni-
      versity of Mississippi Studies in English, 8 (1967),
      7-12.

764   Donald, J. Wallace.   "Reason and the Idea of Man
      in John Ruskin." Dissertation Abstracts, 25 (1963)
      1192 (Columbia).

765   _____ . "Ascidians and Apes: John Ruskin on
      Individual and National Character." Tri-Quarterly,
      8 (1967), 95-106.

766   Dougherty, Charles T.   "Ruskin's Moral Argument.
      Victorian Newsletter, 9 (1948), 4-7.

767   _____ . "Ruskin's Views on Non-Representation-
      al Art." College Art Journal, 15 (Winter 1955),
      112-118.

768   _____ . "Of Ruskin's Gardens." Myth and Sym-
      bol, 15 (1963), 141-151.

769   Edwards, Ralph.   "Ruskin on English Contempo-
      rary Artists." Connoisseur, 144 (Nov. 1959), 91-
      95.

770   Fontaney, Pierre.   "Ruskin and Paradise Re-
      gained." Victorian Studies, 12 (March 1969), 347-
      356.

771 Gleckner, Robert F. "Ruskin and Byron." English Language Notes, 3 (1965), 47-51.

772 Gordon, Jan B. "The Imaginary Portrait: Fin-de-siècle Icon." University of Windsor Review, 5 (Fall 1969), 81-104.

773 Hamilton, K. M. "The Road Back to Ruskin." Hibbert Journal, 49 (Oct. 1951), 48-55.

774 Hobson, J. A. "Ruskin and Democracy." Contemporary Review, 81 (Jan. 1902), 103-112.

775 Janes, G. M. "The Social Ethics of Ruskin." Quarterly Journal of University of North Dakota, 23 (1933).

776 "John Ruskin--Wine Propagandist." Ridley's Wine and Spirit Trade Circular, 1030 (Aug. 14, 1933), 615-619 and 1031 (Sept. 14, 1933), 693-697.

777 Johnson, Alan P. "The Concept of the Italian Renaissance in Early Victorian Literature (1836-60)." Dissertation Abstracts, 28 (1966), 679A (Minnesota).

778 Johnson, Wendell Stacy. "'The Bride of Literature': Ruskin, the Eastlakes, and Mid-Victorian Theories of Art." Victorian Newsletter, 26 (1964), 23-28.

779 Kimbrough, Robert. "Calm Between Crises: Pattern and Direction in Ruskin's Mature Thought." Transcripts of the Wisconsin Academy of Sciences, Arts, and Letters, 49 (1960), 219-227.

780 Landow, George P. "Ruskin and Baudelaire on Art and Artist." University of Toronto Quarterly, 37 (1967-1968), 295-308.

781 _____. "Ruskin's Version of 'Ut Pictura Poesis.'" Journal of Aesthetics and Art Criticism, 26 (Summer 1968), 521-528.

782 _____ . "J. D. Harding and John Ruskin on Nature's Infinite Variety." Journal of Aesthetics and Art Criticism, 27 (Spring 1970), 369-380.

783 Larson, Russell R. "The Idea of Social Structure in the Works of John Ruskin." Dissertation Abstracts, 32 (1970), 6381A-6382A (Michigan).

784 LeRoy, Gaylord C. "Ruskin and 'The Condition of England.'" South Atlantic Quarterly, 47 (Oct. 1948) 534-548.

785 Levi, Olma C. "Ruskin's Views on Poetry." Sewanee Review, 31 (1923), 426-445.

786 Lindsay, Lord. "Ruskin and the Social Conscience. Listener, 41 (April 1948).

787 Lloyd, Michael. "Hawthorne, Ruskin, and the Hostile Tradition." English Miscellany, 6 (1955), 109-133.
    "The Hostile Tradition" toward Italy.

788 McLean, R. S. "Altruistic Ideals Versus Leisure Class Values: An Irreconcilable Conflict in John Ruskin." Journal of Aesthetics and Art Criticism, 30 (Spring 1973), 347-356.

789 Marriott, J. A. R. "Ruskin's Economics." Cornhill Magazine, 127 (April 1923), 403-414.

790 Millett, Kate. "Debate over Women: Ruskin Versus Mill." Victorian Studies, 14 (Spring 1970), 63-82.
    This article also appears in Suffer and Be Still: Women in the Victorian Age. Ed. Martha Vicinus. See Millett, Kate, entry no. 508.

791 Mills, John F. "Ruskin and Burkhardt in Venice During the Renaissance." Criticism, 1 (1959), 139-151.

792 Morris, Bertram. "Ruskin on the Pathetic Fal-

lacy: or On How a Moral Theory of Art May
Fail." Journal of Aesthetics and Art Criticism,
14 (Dec. 1955), 248-266.

793 _____. "Ruskin on the Moral Imagination in
Architecture." University of Colorado Studies in
Language and Literature, 6:39-54.

794 Nash, J. V. "The Utopia of John Ruskin." Open
Court, 45:176-181.

795 Neville, Mary Eileen. "The Function of the Concept of Organic Unity in the Writings of John Ruskin Between 1857 and 1870." Dissertation Abstracts, 20 (1958), 291 (St. Louis University).
    Neville disputes the belief of some scholars that
    John Ruskin abruptly reversed his social philos-
    ophy in 1860. She contends that John Ruskin's
    later works did not spring from a demented
    mind, but were the logical developments of his
    theory of organic unity.

796 Penny, Nicholas. "Ruskin's Ideas on Growth in
Architecture and Ornament." British Journal of
Aesthetics, 13 (Summer 1973), 276-286.

797 Poston, Lawrence Sanford, III. "Five Victorians
on Italian Renaissance Culture: A Problem in Historical Perspectives." Dissertation Abstracts, 25
(1964), 484 (Princeton).
    The "Five Victorians" are John Ruskin, Brown-
    ing, Eliot, Pater, and Symonds.

798 _____. "Ruskin and Browning's Artists." English Miscellany, 15 (1964), 195-212.

799 Reilly, Joseph J. "Ruskin and War." Catholic
World, 152 (Dec. 1940), 267-275.

800 _____. "Ruskin on Love and Marriage." Catholic World, 164 (Dec. 1946), 232-239.

801 Robertson, Mary. "Ruskin on Water Color."

Boston Public Library, 23 (April 1948), 132-134.

802 Roe, F. W. "Ruskin and the Sense of Beauty."
     Wisconsin University Studies in Language and Literature, 2:270-299.

803 Roellinger, Francis X., Jr. "Ruskin on Education." Journal of General Education, 5 (Oct. 1950),
     38-47.

804 Rosenberg, John D. "A Sermon to Soldiers."
     Columbia University Forum, 10 (Spring 1967), 40-
     43.

805 Ross, Malcolm Mackenzie. "Ruskin, Hooker and
     the Christian Theoria." Essays in English Literature from the Renaissance to the Victorian Age,
     20 (1963), 283-303.

806 San Juan, E., Jr. "Ruskin and Exuberance: Control in Literature." Orbis Litterarum, 23 (1968),
     257-264.

807 Sargent, Walter. "Ruskin as a Critic of Art."
     American Magazine of Art, 10 (Aug. 1919), 387-
     392.

808 Seddon, Richard. "Ruskin's Bit of Decadence."
     Apollo, 75 (Jan. 1962), 6-7.

809 Sencourt, Robert. "Turner and Ruskin." Contemporary Review, 181 (Jan. 1952), 34-38.

810 Shaw, Valerie A. "Ruskin and Science." Dissertation Abstracts, 32 (1970), 6943A (Yale).

811 Smallwood, Osborn T. "In Quest of a Faith:
     John Ruskin's Theological Searchings." Cresset,
     13 (1950), 7-13.

812 Spiese, John G. "John Ruskin as a Writer of History." Dissertation Abstracts, 29 (1968), 4441A
     (Pennsylvania State).

813   Stevens, L. Robert. "John Ruskin, God, and the Happening." South Atlantic Quarterly, 71 (Spring 1972), 149-154.

814   Sussman, Herbert. "Hunt, Ruskin, and 'The Scapegoat.'" Victorian Studies, 12 (Sept. 1968), 83-90.

815   Thomas, J. D. "Poetic Truth and Pathetic Fallacy." Texas Studies in Literature and Language, 3 (Autumn 1961), 342-347.

816   Thomas, T. Glyn. "The Relationship of Art to Religion: A Study of John Ruskin." Expository Times, 82 (March 1971), 182-185.

817   Tremaine, George. "Ruskin as Music Critic." Musical Times, 91 (Jan. 1950), 9-10.

818   Unrau, John. "Ruskin's Uses of the Adjective Moral." English Studies, 52 (Aug. 1971), 339-347.

819   "Viewpoints on Architecture." Magazine of Art, 37 (March, 1944), 88.

820   Waller, John O. "Ruskin on Slavery: A Semantic Examination." Victorian Newsletter, 28 (Fall 1965), 13-16.

821   Watson, Francis. "The Devil and Mr. Ruskin." Encounter, 38 (June 1972), 64-70.

822   Wesling, Donald. "Ruskin and the Adequacy of Landscape." Texas Studies in Literature and Language, 9 (Summer 1967), 253-272.

823   Whiting, Frederick A. "Art and Acrimony." Apollo, 98 (July 1973), 43-46.

824   Woollen, C. J. "John Ruskin: Educationalist." Journal of Education, 80 (Nov. 1948), 614.

825   _____. "John Ruskin: Educationalist." Parents' Review, (Nov. 1949), 258-260.

6.   Ruskin Compared to Others

826   Arthos, John. "Ruskin and Tolstoi: 'The Dignity of Man.'" Dalhousie Review, 43 (1963), 5-15.

827   Broderick, J. C. "An Emerson-Ruskin Parallel." Notes and Queries, 1 (1954), 314.

828   Colburn, William E. "Ruskin and Browning: The Poet's Responsibility." Studies in the Literary Imagination, 1 (April 1968), 37-46.

829   Downes, W. H. "John Ruskin and Walter Pach: Defenders of the Faith." American Magazine of Art, 20 (Aug. 1929), 455-459.

830   Gridley, Roy. "Walden and Ruskin's 'The White-Thorn Blossom.'" Emerson Society Quarterly, 26 (1962), 31-34.

831   King, Donald R. "The Vision of 'Being' in Hopkins' Poetry and Ruskin's Modern Painters." Discourse, 9 (1966), 316-324.

832   Laughin, Clare E. "Stories of Authors' Loves: Two Lights that Failed--Ruskin and Fitzgerald." Good Words, (May 1904).

833   Mackerness, E. D. "The Voice of Prophecy: Carlyle and Ruskin." Pelican Guide, 6:294-308.

834   Millhauser, Milton. "The Two Boyhoods." Hartford Studies in Literature, 4:36-51.
      "The Two Boyhoods" are those of John Ruskin and J. S. Mill.

835   Morton, E. P. "Ruskin's Pathetic Fallacy and Keats' Treatment of Nature." Poet Lore, 12 (1900), 58-70.

7. Assessments of Ruskin's Life and Works

a. 19th Century Assessments

836   "John Ruskin." Quarterly Review, 191 (April 1900), 393.

837   Jump, J. D. "Ruskin Satirized, 1857." PMLA, 64 (1949), 597-598.

838   "Life." Chicago Art Institute Scrapbook, 12 (Dec. 1899-July 1900), 19.

839   Memorabilist. "Arnold on Ruskin: and Henry James." Notes and Queries, 185 (1943), 17.

840   Statham, Henry Heathcote. "The Truth About Ruskin." Fortnightly Review, (March 1900).

841   Townsend, Francis G. "The American Estimate of Ruskin, 1847-1860." Philological Quarterly, 32 (1953), 69-82.

b. 20th Century Assessments

842   Banyard, Grace. "Ruskin." Fortnightly, 172 (Feb. 1950), 112-118.

843   Bentley, John A. "Ruskin as a Literary Critic." Harvard University Summaries of Theses, (1930), 186-189.

844   Burd, Van Akin. "Ruskin, Rossetti, and William Bell Scott: A Second Arrangement." Philological Quarterly, 48 (Jan. 1969), 102-107.

845   Bush-Brown, Albert. "'Get an Honest Bricklayer!': The Scientist's Answer to Ruskin." Journal of

Aesthetics and Art Criticism, 16 (March 1958), 348-356.

846   "Can Ruskin Be Saved?" Industrial Design, 13 (March 1966), 25.

847   Cornforth, John. "A Resurrection of Ruskin." Country Life, 135 (Jan. 23, 1964), 170-171. Arts Council exhibition.

848   Curtin, Frank D. "Ruskin in French Criticism: A Possible Reappraisal." PMLA, 77 (1962), 199-245.

849   Dawson, A. M. P. "A Victorian Prophet with a Message for Today." Hibbert Journal, 45 (1947), 253-267.

850   Dearden, James S. "Ruskin Galleries, Bembridge School, Isle of Wight." Apollo, 75 (Dec. 1961), 178-181.

851   _____. "The Ruskin Galleries at Bembridge School, Isle of Wight." The Bulletin of the John Rylands Library, 51 (Spring 1969), 310-347.

852   _____. "Ruskin's Politics by Bernard Shaw." Book Collector, 20 (Autumn 1971), 335-346.

853   Dougherty, Charles T. "John Ruskin." Victorian Newsletter, 14 (1950), 23-24.

854   Evans, Joan. "John Ruskin: New Conclusions." Art News, 53 (Sept. 1954), 28-29.

855   "Follies--But No Fool." Times Literary Supplement, 63 (March 5, 1964), 195.

856   Grigson, Geoffrey. "Pope of Art." New Statesman, 67 (Feb. 7, 1964), 222-223.

857   "John Ruskin: Prose Painter." Times Literary Supplement, 71 (Nov. 10, 1972), 1353-1354.

858   "John Ruskin Returns to Verona. " Connoisseur,
       163 (Sept. 1966), 23.

859   Litzenberg, Karl.   "Controversy over Ruskin: A
       Review Article. " Journal of English and Germanic
       Philology, 50 (1951), 529-531.

860   Livingstone, R. W.   "Ruskin. " Proceedings of
       the British Academy, 31 (1948), 85-102.

861   Lunn, Arnold.   "Ruskin. " Dublin Review, (1951),
       98-114.

862   McDill, H. C.   "Why the Ruskin Colony Failed. "
       Gunton's Magazine, 22 (1902).

863   "Portrait. " Ciba Review, 11 (May 1958), 5.

864   "Proust on Ruskin: Excerpts. " Architectural Re-
       view, 112 (July 1952), 61.

865   Rosenberg, John D.   "Voice in the Wilderness:
       A Study of John Ruskin. " Dissertation Abstracts,
       26 (1960), 3308 (Columbia).

866   "'Ruskin and His Circle': A Comprehensive Exhi-
       bition Arranged by the Arts Council. " Illustrated
       London News, 244 (Feb. 1, 1964), 169.

867   "Ruskin Memorial Number. " The Bookman, 17
       (March 1900).

868   "Ruskin the Artist: Exhibition at Leighton House
       in Kensington. " Connoisseur, 135 (April 1955),
       115.

869   Russell, John.   "Ruskin the Lost Leader. " Art in
       America, 52 (June 1964), 132-133.

870   Rutherston, Albert Daniel.   "Ruskin Drawing
       School Collection in the Ashmolean Museum. " Art-
       work, 7 (1931), 36-44.

871   Seddon, Richard. "Full Circle: Arts Council Exhibition." Guardian, (Jan. 23, 1964), 8.

872   Tawney, R. H. "John Ruskin." Observer, (Feb. 19, 1919).
       Reprinted in The Radical Tradition. Ed. Rita Hinden. See Tawney, R. H., entry no. 539.

873   Williams-Ellis, Amabel. "Why Bother about Ruskin?" Saturday Review of Literature, 10 (Dec. 1933), 379.

8.   Items

874   Borrie, M. A. F. "The Cockerell Papers." British Museum Quarterly, 30 (1966), 88-93.

875   Bracken, Julia M. "Plaque." Chicago Art Institute Scrapbook, 13 (Aug. 1900-March 1901), 92.

876   Briggs, R. C. H. "I Am, Sir, Your Obedient Servant." Journal of the William Morris Society, 2 (1926), 18-27.

877   Burd, V. A. "The Winnington Papers." Victorian Newsletter, 18 (Nov. 1955), 4-5.

878   Cave, Oenone. "Story of Reticella." Handweaver and Craftsman, 11 (Summer 1960), 14-16.

879   "Editorial: The Pleasant Place of All Festivity." Apollo, 94 (Sept. 1971), 171.

880   Ferriday, Peter. "Oxford Museum." Architectural Review, 132 (Dec. 1962), 408-416.

881   Fleming, Gordon H. "That Ne'er Shall Meet Again." Times Literary Supplement, 71 (Jan. 21, 1972), 69.
       A debate about John Ruskin and Millais, and

about Fleming's sources for his work, followed
this publication in the letters section of the
Times Literary Supplement. The letters ap-
peared as follows:
Lutyens, Mary. 71 (Jan. 28, 1972), 99.
Dearden, James S. 71 (Jan. 28, 1972), 99.
Surtees, Virginia. 71 (Jan. 28, 1972), 99.
Fredeman, William E. 71 (March 24, 1972), 337.
Richards, Bernard. 71 (April 28, 1972), 496.
Fleming, Gordon H. 71 (April 28 1972), 496.

882 Gage, J. "Turner and Stourhead: The Making of
a Classicist?" Art Quarterly, 37 (Spring 1974),
59-87.

883 Hitchcock, Henry Russell. "Ruskin and Butter-
field." Architectural Review, 116 (Nov. 1954),
285-289.

884 Hollyer, F. "Portraits." Architectural Review,
7 (1900), 49.

885 Kossatz, Horst Herbert. "Vienna Secession and
Its Early Relations with Great Britain." Studio
International, 181 (Jan. 1971), 9.

886 Lutyens, Mary. "Portraits of Effie." Apollo, 87
(March 1968), 190.

887 McClelland, V. A. "Ruskin's Apologia." Down-
side Review, 255:128-134.

888 Meeson, Philip. "Drawing, Art and Education."
British Journal of Aesthetics, 12 (Summer 1972),
276-289.

889 Reid, Jane Davidson. "True Judith: Botticelli's
Judith." Art Journal, 28 (Summer 1969), 376-378.

890 Rosenthal, T. G. "To Praise or Not to Damn."
Listener, 71 (Jan. 30, 1964), 202.

891 "Ruskin Gold Medal Controversy." Royal Institute

of British Architects Journal, 70 (April 1963), 165-167.

892   "Sculpture Exhibit at the Chicago Art Institute."
        Monumental News, 18 (Jan. 1906), 21.

893   "Simple Blue Country." Architectural Review, 79
        (May 1936), 247-248.

894   Sinclair, W.   "The Ruskin Museum at Sheffield."
        International Studio, 36 (Dec. 1908), 127-131.

895   "Victorian Cross-Currents." Apollo, 85 (Jan.
        1967), 5.

C. REPRODUCTIONS OF VISUAL ART

896 "Abbeville." Connoisseur, 103 (June 1939), 353.

897 "Aiguilles." Art News, 54 (Dec. 1955), 27.

898 "Amalfi." Gazette des Beaux-Arts, 80 (Dec. 1972), 25.

899 "Belaggio." Apollo, 79 (April 1964), lxi, and "From Belaggio." lxi.

900 "Belaggio." Apollo, 85 (June 1967), cxxxvi.

901 "British Watercolors and Drawings." Rhode Island School of Design Bulletin, 58 (April 1972), 58-60. "Pass of Faido, St. Gothard," attributed to John Ruskin. Includes, also: "In the Alps," "Spray of Juniper Berries," and "Study of a Hawthorn in Flower."

902 "Castelbarco Tomb, Verona." Burlington Magazine, 108 (Aug. 1966), iii, and in Burlington Magazine, 108 (Sept. 1966), xxx.

903 "Coast Scene Near Dunbar." Connoisseur, 180 (Aug. 1972), 315.

904 "Court of the Ducal Palace." Apollo, 88 (Nov. 1968), 88.

905 Dearden, James S. "The Cunliffe Collection of Ruskin Drawings." The Connoisseur, 171 (Aug. 1969), 237-240.

906   "Interior of the Church of San Frediano, Lucca."
       Country Life, 153 (Feb. 1 1973), 267.

907   "J. M. W. Turner as He Was Dressed for His
       Visit to the Opening of the Royal Academy."
       Studio, 171 (June 1966), 264.

908   "Landscape Near Bellinzona." Apollo, 85 (March
       1967), xcvi.

909   "Loggia of the Ducal Palace." Pencil Points, 12
       (Jan. 1931), 10.

910   "Mer de Glace, Chamonix." Gazette des Beaux-
       Arts, 73 (Feb. 1969), 98.

911   "Mont Blanc." Connoisseur, 172 (Dec. 1969), 172.

912   "Naples" and "Quattro Fontane, Rome." Apollo,
       79 (Feb. 1964), xxi.

913   "Pisa." Studio, 160 (Nov. 1960), 190.

914   "Rocky Landscape." Connoisseur, 185 (March
       1974), 111.

915   "St. Gothard Pass, Near Amsteg." Brooklyn Mu-
       seum Quarterly, 20 (Oct. 1933), 93.

916   "Study of a Scotch Fir." Connoisseur, 165 (June
       1967), lxxxii.

917   "Teal." Art News, 63 (Feb. 1965), 4.

918   "View of an Old House in Fribourg." Apollo, 96
       (July 1972), 17.

919   "Watercolor Copy of Detail from Botticelli's Paint-
       ing 'Moses and Jethro's Daughter at the Well.'"
       Journal of the Warburg and Courtald Institutes, 23
       (July 1960), opposite page 296.

920   "Zipporah." Apollo, 82 (Aug. 1965), 121.

PART III

NON-ENGLISH LANGUAGE WORKS ON JOHN RUSKIN AND TRANSLATIONS INTO NON-ENGLISH LANGUAGES:

A Selective Listing

A. FRENCH

1. Books

921 Autret, Jean. L'influence de Ruskin sur la vie, les idées et l'oeuvre de Marcel Proust. Genève: Librairie Droz, 1955, and Lille: Librairie Giard, 1955.
Autret has also written about John Ruskin in English. See Autret, Jean. Ruskin and the French, entry no. 267.

922 Bardoux, J. Le Mouvement Idéaliste et Social dans la Littérature anglaise au xixe siècle: John Ruskin. 2nd edition. Paris: Calmann-Levy, 1901.

923 Bruhnès, H. J. Ruskin et la Bible: pour servir à l'histoire d'une pensée. Paris: Perrin, 1901.

924 Chevrillon, A. La Pensée de Ruskin. Paris: Hachette, 1909.

925 _____. "La jeunesse de Ruskin." Nouvelle études anglaises. Paris: Hachette, 1910, pp. 79-129.

926 Danel, J. Les idées sociales de Ruskin. Paris: Lille, 1912.

927 Delattre, F. Ruskin et Bergson: de l'intuition esthétique à l'intuition métaphysique. London: Oxford University Press, 1947.

928   De Souza, S.   L'influence de Ruskin sur Proust.
      Montpellier: 1932.

929   Fernand-Hue, G.   Ruskin et la femme.   Paris:
      Société Française d'Imprimerie et de Librairie,
      1902.

930   Gally, H.   Ruskin et l'esthétique intuitive.   Paris:
      1933.

931   Jaudel, Philippe.   La Pensée Social de John Rus-
      kin.   Paris: M. Didier, 1973.

932   Lemaitre, Hélene.   Les Pierres dans l'oeuvre de
      Ruskin.   Caen: Faculté des Lettres et Sciences
      Humaines de l'Université, 1965.

933   Maurois, André.   "Proust et Ruskin."   Essays
      and Studies by Members of the Association.   Vol.
      17.   London: Oxford University Press (for the
      English Association), 1910-1933, pp. 25-32.

934   Milsand, J.   L'Esthétique anglaise: Étude sur Mr.
      John Ruskin.   2nd ed.   Lausanne: Frankfurter,
      1906.   (First ed. , 1864.)

935   Proust, Marcel.   Pastiches et mélanges.   Paris:
      1927.
          See Proust, Marcel.   Marcel Proust: A Selec-
      tion from His Miscellaneous Writings.   Trans.
      Gerard Hopkins, entry no. 521.

936   Ruskin, John.   La Couronne d'olivier sauvage, Les
      sept lampes de l'architecture, trans. George El-
      wall.   Paris: Société d'édition artistique, 1900.
      Reprinted: Paris: H. Laurens, 1916.

937   _____ .   Unto this Last, ed. Abbé E. Peltier.
      Paris: G. Beauchesne, 1902.

938   _____ .   La Bible d'Amiens, trans. Marcel
      Proust.   Paris: Mercure de France, 1904.

939 _____ . Les Matins à Florence, trans. Eugenie
Nypels. Paris: H. Laurens, 1906.

940 _____ . Sésame et les lys, trans. Marcel
Proust. Paris: Mercure de France, 1906.

941 _____ . Les Pierres de Venise, trans. Mathilde
P. Crémieux. Paris: H. Laurens, 1906.

942 _____ . La Nature du Gothique, trans. Mathilde
P. Crémieux. Paris: Aillaud, 1907.

943 _____ . Le Repos de Saint-Marc, trans. K.
Johnston. Paris: Hachette, 1908.

944 _____ . Conférences sur l'architecture et la
peinture, ed. E. Cammaerts. Paris: H. Laurens,
1909.

945 _____ . Le Val d'Arno, ed. E. Cammaerts.
Paris: H. Laurens, 1911.

946 _____ . Praeterita, trans. Gaston Paris.
Paris: Hachette, 1911.

947 _____ . Les Peintres modernes, trans. E. Cammaerts. Paris: H. Laurens, 1914.

2. Periodicals

948 Audra, E. "L'influence de Ruskin en France."
Revue des Cours et Conférences, 27 (Jan. 15,
1926), 265-288.

949 Betirac, P. "Justice et Économie Politique:
'Unto this Last' de John Ruskin." Cahiers de
l'Isea, (April 1966), 191-218.

950 Carré, J. M. "L'Italie de Goethe, de Ruskin et

de Taine." Revue de Littérature Comparée, 25
(July 1951), 304-307.

951   Fontaney, Pierre. "Ruskin d'après des livres
       nouveaux." Etudes Anglaises, 13 (Jan.-March
       1960), 32-37.

952   Francastel, Pierre. "La Venise de Ruskin et les
       archéologues." Venezia nelle letterature moderne,
       11:202-211.

953   Guilloux, P. "Les idées d'un réformateur poete,
       Ruskin et la Société moderne." Etudes, 238
       (1923).

954   Kolb, Philip. "Proust et Ruskin: Nouvelles per-
       spectives." Cahiers de l'Association Internationale
       des Etudes Françaises, 12:259-273.

955   Le Breton, Georges. "La folie de Ruskin." Mer-
       cure de France, 349 (Nov. 1963), 615-619.

956   Polis, T. V. 'W. Morris et J. Ruskin (Uiliam
       Morris i Djon Reskin)." Annales Scientifiques des
       "Agrégés" de l'Université de Lithuanie (Outchionyie
       Zapiski Aspirantov Latvian Universiteta), 5 (1966),
       105-135.

957   Proust, Marcel. "John Ruskin." Chronique des
       arts et de la curiosité, (Jan. 27, 1900), 35-36.

958   _____. "Pèlerinages ruskiniens en France."
       Le Figaro, (Feb. 13, 1900).

959   _____. "Ruskin à Notre-Dame d'Amiens."
       Mercure de France, 34 (April 1900), 56-88.

960   _____. "John Ruskin." Gazette des Beaux-
       Arts, 23 (April 1900), 310-318, and 24 (Aug. 1900),
       135-146.

961   _____. "La Bible d'Amiens." Renaissance
       Latine, (Feb. 15, 1903), 314-345, and (March 15,

1903), 620-643.

962 _____ . "Les Trésors des rois." Les Arts de
la Vie, 3 (March 1905), 171-186; (April 1905), 248-
256; and (May 1905), 312-319.

963 Ronci, Gilberto. "Ruskin et l'art Vénitien." Les
Arts Plastiques, 6 (Oct.-Dec. 1953), 365-370.

964 Valette, J. "Lettres Anglo-Saxonnes: Les Jour-
naux de Ruskin." Mercure de France, 338 (May
1960), 135-138.

B. ITALIAN

965 Bartello, Marc. "San Marco e la critica di Ruskin." L'arte, 30 (May-Aug. 1927), 105-118.

966 Mullaly, Terence. Ruskin a Verona: Catalogo.
Verona: Museo di Castelvecchio, 1966.
    Exhibition catalogue.

967 Olivero, F. "Sul 'Saint Mark's Rest' di John Ruskin." Ateneo Veneto, (1909), 237-247.

968 Stegagno, G. B. "Giovanni Ruskin." Madonna
Verona, (1919), 51-52.

969 Zeppieri, Carmine. "Robert de Sizeranne fra Ruskin e Proust." Studi Urbinati di Storia, Filosofia
e Letteratura, 45 (1971), 1137-1150.

970 Zolla, Elmire. "John Ruskin come Goethe vit-
toriano." Cononscenza religiosa, 2 (1971), 188-
200.

C. GERMAN

971   Claus, Paul. "Die Ethik John Ruskins." Die
      Neueren Sprache, 16 (1908).

972   Meyer, J. J. de L.   "John Ruskin und sein Kreis,
      zur Ausstellung des Arts Council of Great Britain
      in London." Das Kunstwerk, 18 (July 1964), 82-
      87.

973   Morlang, Wilhelm.   Die beziehungen zwischen
      Kunst und Religion in den Werken John Ruskin.
      Marburg: Bauer, 1934.

974   von Bunsen, Marie.   John Ruskin, sein Leben und
      sein Werken. Leipzig: Hermann Seemann, 1903.

D. OTHERS

975   Gómez de la Serna, Ramón.   "Ruskin el apasio-
      nado." Efigies.   Madrid: Ediciones Oriente, 1929,
      pp. 223-277.

976   Mollerup, A.   John Ruskin: ˙Hovedtanker I Hans
      Vaeker. Copenhagen: Forlagt af V. Pios Boghan-
      del, 1911.

977   Morton, A. L.   "John Ruskin a Komuna Paryska."
      Przeglad Humanistyczny, 8 (1964), 61-66.

INDEX

Authors, Editors, and Translators